ENVIRONMENT, SPACE, PLACE

VOLUME 9 / ISSUE 2 / FALL 2017

Environment, Space, Place (ISSN 2066-5377) is published twice a year in the spring and fall by the University of Minnesota Press, 111 Third Avenue South, Suite 290, Minneapolis, MN 55401-2520. http://www.upress.umn.edu

Postmaster: Send address changes to *Environment, Space, Place*, University of Minnesota Press, 111 Third Avenue South, Suite 290, Minneapolis, MN 55401-2520.

Essays (between 6,000 and 10,000 words) should be prepared using *Chicago Manual of Style* endnotes. Authors' names should not appear on manuscripts; instead, please include a separate document with the author's name and address and the title of the article and an abstract with your electronic submission. Authors should not refer to themselves in the first person in the submitted text or notes if such references would identify them; any necessary references to the author's previous work, for example, should be in the third person. Submissions and editorial queries should be sent to paddockt1@southernct.edu or heidkampc1@southernct.edu.

Books or films for review should be addressed to
Jeffrey Webb
Review Editor, *Environment, Space, Place*
Department of History & Political Science
Huntington University
2303 College Avenue
Huntington, IN 46750

Address subscription orders, changes of address, and business correspondence (including requests for permission and advertising orders) to *Environment, Space, Place*, University of Minnesota Press, 111 Third Avenue South, Suite 290, Minneapolis, MN 55401-2520.

Subscriptions: Regular rates, U.S.: individual, 1 year, $35; libraries, 1 year, $180. Outside the U.S. add $5 for each year's subscription. Checks should be made payable to the University of Minnesota Press. Back issues are $17.50 for individuals, $90 for libraries (plus $6 shipping for the first copy, $1.25 for each additional copy inside the U.S.; $9.50 shipping for the first copy, $6 for each additional copy, outside the U.S.). *Environment, Space, Place* is available online through the JSTOR Current Scholarship Program at http://jstor.org/r/umnpress.

ENVIRONMENT, SPACE, PLACE

VOLUME 9 / ISSUE 2 / FALL 2017

Book Reviews

Shores of Enlightenment

George Berkeley and the Moral Geography of Hybrid Nature

CHRISTOPHER L. PASTORE

Abstract

This paper examines the American sojourn of the Enlightenment philosopher and theologian George Berkeley. While living in coastal Rhode Island between 1729 and 1731, Berkeley penned his longest philosophical tract, Alciphron: Or, the Minute Philosopher *(1732), which criticized "freethinking," mechanical conceptions of nature in favor of those that emphasized God's providence. To illustrate these two ways of knowing nature, Berkeley, a careful prose stylist, evoked nearby coastal landscapes for contrast. Accordingly, his work broke down dichotomies between ideas and matter and, by extension, culture and nature, which could, this paper argues, inform an environmental ethic for a "hybrid" world.*

"I was never more agreeably surprised than at the first sight of the town and its harbour," wrote George Berkeley of his arrival in Newport, Rhode Island, on January 23, 1729.[1] The 43-year-old Dean of Derry in northern Ireland and the highest-ranking Anglican official ever to visit New England had spent four and a half months "blundering about the Ocean" aboard the 250-ton *Lucy*, followed by a short stay in Virginia, and then a long slog up the coast against the prevailing winds of winter. Berkeley noted that his wife, Anne Forster, whom he had married only a few weeks before departing England, was "much hurt and weakened" by seasickness during the voyage, her discomfort likely made more acute by pregnancy.[2] Nevertheless, when they arrived in Newport, she received "wonderful relief" and Berkeley, an esteemed member of London's most fashionable literary circles, was warmly welcomed among the town's elite.[3] So eager to meet Berkeley was Trinity Church Rector James Honeyman that it has been said he adjourned his Sunday service and escorted his flock to the docks.[4] As the only Episcopal clergyman on Aquidneck Island, Honeyman opened his home to the Dean and his wife. Berkeley's impression of Newport's principal parson was so favorable that he called Honeyman "a person of very good sense and merit on all accounts," which was, he admitted, "much more than I expected to have found in this place."[5]

For Berkeley, the city perched at the mouth of Narragansett Bay was full of pleasant surprises. Bustling with ship traffic and well on its way to becoming one of the largest cities in British North America, Newport shimmered with the polish of prosperity.[6] So appealing were his new surroundings, that Berkeley, who had intended to build a seminary in Bermuda, began to rethink his plans.[7] Although he had received an official crown charter and a promise of £20,000, the money, mired in the bogs of British bureaucracy, was less than forthcoming. He had also faced sharp criticism from Anglican missionaries who had been to Bermuda and deemed his proposal untenable.[8] Heeding the advice of his friend Henry Newman, who was originally from Rehoboth, Massachusetts, along the northeast shores of Narragansett Bay, Berkeley set out to realize his dream in Rhode Island.[9]

Both materially and metaphorically, Berkeley predicated his American mission on the currents of an expanding Atlantic world. In his original proposal for what he planned to call St. Paul's College, he had argued that "rivulets perpetually issuing forth from a fountain or reservoir of learning and religion, and streaming through all parts of America must in due time have a great effect, in purging away the ill manners and irreligion of our Colonies." He took particular pains to emphasize the importance of his proposed seminary's remote island setting, "where its waters, out of the way of anything that may corrupt them, remain clear and pure."[10] That Berkeley saw among the waters of the western Atlantic a source of imperial redemption was no coincidence. In its cleansing Christian symbolism and fluid, mixing nature water had come to reflect Berkeley's way of imagining the shifting currents of eighteenth-century philosophical thought. While his writings bristled at the notion that science could ever supplant religious tradition, Berkeley nevertheless recognized that these two ways of knowing the natural world had begun and would continue to converge.

Echoing Berkeley's ideas, recent scholarship on the Enlightenment has shown that religion and natural philosophy developed not in opposition to each other but hand-in-hand. As J. G. A Pocock explained, the Enlightenment was "a product of religious debate and not merely a rebellion against it."[11] Similarly, David Sorkin, resisting what he called a "secular master narrative," argued that "the Enlightenment was not only compatible with religious belief but conducive to it."[12] So firmly entangled were early modern theology and natural philosophy that Sarah Rivett has identified a "science of the soul," which she argued preceded or at the very least was mutually constitutive with experimental philosophy.[13] Put another way, the Enlightenment was not simply an outcome—a more rational, scientific understanding of the world—but a process, one in which nature was continuously reevaluated (and redefined) as old beliefs mixed with the new.

Berkeley waded into this mix and described its details. Layered with many meanings, "nature" in seventeenth- and eighteenth-century terms evoked both the material world and a shifting set of assumptions about the ways humans interacted with it and each other. At once a mechanical system and a set of moral directives, nature, it was widely acknowledged, operated according to laws, the author of which (and the extent of his contribution) was hotly contested. The shifting significance of and manifold explanations for the term nature has in some cases encouraged scholars to narrow their inquiries to either nature's material qualities or to the history of ideas.[14] In other cases, it has encouraged them to differentiate between "pristine" environments and those that have been shaped or sullied by human action. But those firm distinctions have begun to erode. Taking stock of the current state of environmental history, Paul Sutter recently concluded that a new generation of scholars has begun to examine "hybrid" landscapes that deny the "polar categories of nature and culture—and the simple but powerful moral narratives that such bifurcation facilitated—for approaches that see all environments as interweaving the natural and the cultural in complex ways."[15]

A closer look at the philosopher and theologian George Berkeley, a keen observer of and commentator on the myriad meanings of early modern nature, reveals that hybrid environments have long come to reflect powerful moral narratives of their own. The eighteenth century saw the systemization of natural knowledge, the reevaluation of religious beliefs and human relations, and the growing impulse to expand and refine imperial domains, all of which created a new set of assumptions about the human place in nature.[16] Although the careful study of human-nature "hybridity" has pushed environmental history in new directions, scholars, Sutter insists, "must better contend with and communicate the cultural, material, and moral complexity implicated in the term."[17] This paper attempts to do just that. By examining the age of Enlightenment when these hybrid notions of nature were first constructed, and by narrowing our focus to Berkeley, widely considered the ultimate "constructionist," we can begin to parse the moral complexities that have come to shape our modern relationship to and interaction with the natural world.

A careful textual analysis of Berkeley's most prominent published works, moreover, reveals the extent to which these changing notions of nature were firmly entangled with contemporary conceptions of landscape.[18] If by the beginning of the eighteenth century Cartesian philosophy had divided the material realm from the mental, Berkeley used imagery of coastal spaces in his prose to show that ideas and matter were inextricably connected.[19] Similarly, if some believed that religious orthodoxy opposed human progress, the careful poet used imagery to illustrate their interdependence. For the good Dean, matter flowed seamlessly into the realm of ideas, Christian morality underpinned progress, and nature as God guided it was something continually renewed.[20] Indeed, Berkeley's definition of progress—one that eschewed excess and honored restraint, that sought harmony between nature and culture, and that emphasized the consanguinity of ideas and matter—leads us one step closer toward understanding the moral complexities of hybridity.

Berkeley opens a window into the complex ways in which God, natural philosophy, the human imagination, and the material world came to constitute a new definition of nature during the age of Enlightenment. Ranked alongside John Locke and David Hume as one of the most influential British "empiricists" (those who believed knowledge was not innate but acquired through the senses), Berkeley was nevertheless an "idealist" who believed that the world around him had no material foundation. Rather, according to Berkeley's doctrine of "immaterialism" it was God who continually projected images of things like rivers, rocks, forests, and oceans onto the human mind. Nature was not something manifested in matter, but rather a product of perception. And those representations of reality were in perennial flux.

This ebb and flow of ideas shaped the way Berkeley the philosopher and rhetorician imagined and represented the world. A man of bold imperial ambition and deep, abiding faith, Berkeley saw in America a means of reconciling earthly progress with God's eternal grace. In consequence, the land and seascapes near what would become his Aquidneck Island home inspired and provided the setting for his longest philosophical tract, *Alciphron: Or, the Minute Philosopher* (1732), which denied the legitimacy of "freethinking," mechanical conceptions of nature in favor of those that emphasized divine Providence. But in its deep disdain for deism and earnest defense of orthodoxy, Berkeley's work, like that of many other "natural theologians," nevertheless acknowledged and dramatized the ways these competing conceptions of nature overlapped.[21] As Steven Mentz has shown, early modern literary culture typically depicted the land as "orderly and human" while the sea was "chaotic and divine."[22] Accordingly, Berkeley framed his arguments about the natural world and the human and spiritual forces

Figure 1. George Berkeley before his departure to America. He points toward a redemptive sea. John Smibert, *Bishop George Berkeley*, 1727. National Portrait Gallery, Smithsonian Institution; gift of the Morris and Gwendolyn Cafritz Foundation; Frame conserved with funds from the Smithsonian Women's Committee.

that shaped it along the ocean's edge. In floating his idea for a seminary from one island to another, the eminent Anglican, iconoclastic philosopher, and literary luminary played an important role in shaping a definition of nature that wedded the material world with the human imagination and, by extension, nature with culture. In the process, Berkeley began to construct a moral geography for a hybrid world.

EDDIES OF ENLIGHTENMENT

If Bermuda's beautiful weather and prime location at the crossroads of Atlantic communication had initially assured Berkeley that he would "spend the residue of [his] days" there, Rhode Island's garden-like appearance and near-constant ship traffic convinced him that perhaps he had stumbled upon a suitable alternative.[23] So taken with Rhode Island was Berkeley that within a month of his arrival, he wrote, "I should not demure one moment about situating our College here."[24] Having purchased a 96-acre farm next door to Honeyman's, Berkeley observed in April 1729 that "The climate is like that of Italy, tho' not quite so cold in the winter as I have known it in many places north of Rome." He explained that the spring came later in Rhode Island, but that the "fields are now green and the trees budded," although the leaves had not yet "shot forth." Underlying such dramatic seasonal changes was Aquidneck Island's striking physical landscape. "The face of the country," he wrote, "is pleasantly laid out in hills vales woods and rising grounds, watered with several rivulets." His property had "two fine groves" and a small river, which winding toward the shore, unveiled "very amusing rocky scenes, and fine landschapes [sic] of the sea intermixed with capes and islands."[25] The paradise he had imagined in Bermuda unfolded before him on Aquidneck. So rich was the land that he noted "vines sprout up of themselves to an extraordinary size, and seem as natural to this soil as to any I ever saw." Well-watered and crawling with cattle, Newport, which contained "about six thousand souls," was, in Berkeley's estimation, "the most thriving flourishing place in all America for its bigness."[26]

Among the coastal gardens of Aquidneck Island, Berkeley began sowing the seeds of his school. After signing the deed on his farm, Berkeley broke ground on his home during the spring of 1729. Although it is unclear whether he modified the existing house and stable or tore them down and started anew, he nevertheless commenced construction of a stately, two-story saltbox, replete with sitting rooms befitting a man of prominence. He filled them with fine furniture and fifty-five cases of books containing upwards of 2,000 volumes.[27] The fireplaces were decorated with hand-painted Dutch tiles.[28] Although it was wrapped in the clapboards of the country, the building was carefully proportioned in Palladian style, its central doorway flanked by ionic pilasters and topped by an elegant triangular tympanum. Unabashed in his ambition to bring the religious arm of imperial power to the periphery, Berkeley named his new home Whitehall after what had been the royal palace in London during most of the sixteenth and seventeenth centuries.[29]

Comfortably situated and still waiting for the purse strings to loosen in London, Berkeley shifted his attention elsewhere during the fall of 1729. His wife had given birth to a son that spring.[30] Throughout the summer he had preached almost every Sunday at Trinity Church in Newport and maintained frequent correspondence with friends in England and Ireland.[31] But as the leaves of Aquidneck turned and the air grew cool, he appeared less frequently and his correspondence slowed. Alas, winter fell across southern New England and hardened. Boston saw more snow in January than it had in nearly fifteen years.[32] Sitting by the fire at Whitehall, Berkeley, with nothing else to do except wait and hope and write, "passed the winter," he later explained, "in a profound solitude."[33] Surrounded by windblown fields and the silent coves just beyond them, Berkeley began to compose his longest philosophical work, *Alciphron: Or, the Minute Philosopher*. Although the book was set ostensibly in the English countryside, the descriptions of local landmarks placed it undoubtedly on Aquidneck Island. His opening lines, moreover, explained, "I have enjoyed such liberty and leisure in this distant retreat, far beyond that verge of the great whirlpool of business, faction, and pleasure, which is called the world."[34] Quietly hiding among the extremities of the empire, Berkeley set out to define nature in the broadest sense of the term. But when he inked his quill and described Rhode Island, the Dean of Derry stirred a maelstrom of Enlightenment debate along the shores of southern New England.

A dedicated student and precocious thinker, Berkeley began his journey toward philosophical fame when he was still quite young. The eldest of six sons, he grew up in a middling but well-connected family in the town of Kilkenny, Ireland, roughly seventy miles southwest of Dublin, where his father, William, was most likely a royalist revenue collector.[35] When George was eleven he entered Kilkenny College, and then in the year 1700, at fifteen years old, matriculated at Trinity College in Dublin, where he completed his B.A. degree four years later.[36] He remained in Dublin and in 1707 earned the position of Fellow, whereupon he continued his studies, earning an M.A. in 1707, and a B.D. and D.D. in 1721, while also serving as a tutor and lecturer. It was during his tenure at Trinity that he published his *Essay Toward a New Theory of Vision* (1709). A year later, he was ordained into the Anglican Church and then published a second book titled *A Treatise Concerning the Principles of Human Knowledge*. Although both volumes elicited sharp criticism, they also earned him recognition from some of the leading minds of the time as well as the favor of church officials. After seventeen years of service at Trinity College, in 1724 he left to become the Dean of Derry.[37]

Berkeley's early works were contentious because they challenged some of the most important findings of the Scientific Revolution. Chafing at the ways advances in natural knowledge had served to mechanize the material world, Berkeley argued that nature should be understood not in terms of parts or systems but in its divine totality. Underpinning Berkeley's philosophy of nature was his doctrine of "immaterialism," which denied the existence of physical matter independent of the mind. The world, he argued, consisted only of ideas, which wafted on the breath of God into the minds of mankind. Material reality did not exist independent of Providence. Particularly grating for Berkeley was what he saw as the "skepticism" and "atheism" of some of the seventeenth century's leading thinkers. Such luminaries as Thomas Hobbes, René Descartes, John Locke, and Robert Boyle were known to believe in a creator, but held that material reality existed independent of divine intervention.[38] Famously comparing nature to the Strasbourg glockenspiel, Boyle, who laid the foundations of modern chemistry, explained that the world was "like a clock" that "once set a-moving, all things proceed according to the artificer's first design." The "little statues," he explained, "do not require (like those of puppets) the peculiar interposing of the artificer or any intelligent agent employed by him, but perform their functions upon particular occasions by virtue of the general and primitive contrivance of the whole engine."[39] God had created the world, Boyle argued, but once it was set in motion, the designer no longer meddled in its daily operation. For Berkeley, conversely, God's absence, even if only for a moment, undermined the very foundations of reality. Without his continuous tinkering, without a steady flood of grace, the world would undoubtedly vanish. "[R]eal things," Berkeley concluded in his *Principles of Human Knowledge*, were simply "ideas imprinted on the sense by the Author of Nature."[40]

Berkeley's world was but a mirage of the mind—one that his critics believed he had completely lost. Sir John Percival, Berkeley's close friend, wrote that a physician with whom he was acquainted "argued you must needs be mad, and that you ought to take remedies." A bishop, presumably in London where Percival was writing, "pitied" Berkeley. Percival's wife wanted to know that if there "be nothing but spirit and ideas," then how should one consider the "six days' creation that preceded man[?]"[41] Dr. Samuel Clarke, The Rector at St. James, claimed that Berkeley was a "fair arguer, and a clear writer," but that his "first principles" were "false." The Earl of Pembroke applauded Berkeley's efforts but admitted he "could not be convinced of the non-existence of matter."[42]

Firm in his convictions, Berkeley reworked his thesis, which he published in 1713 as *The Three Dialogues Between Hylas and Philonous*. To clarify his arguments he employed Platonic dialogues, or polemical debates couched in casual conversation, which earned his new book and the ideas in it wider recognition.[43] The writer Richard Steele embraced Berkeley's philosophy and accessible prose and hired him to refute "free thinkers" in his newspaper, the *Guardian*. Berkeley befriended Joseph Addison, whom he praised for having the same "peculiar delicacy and easiness of writing" as Steele but who was also "a great philosopher, having applied himself to speculative studies more than any of the wits that I know." With Jonathan Swift, "one of the best natured and agreeable men in the world," Berkeley developed an enduring friendship.[44] So taken with Berkeley was Swift that he recommended him as chaplain and secretary to the Earl of Peterborough, with whom Berkeley traveled through France and Italy from October 1713 to August 1714 and again from 1716 to 1720.[45] While in France, Berkeley penned his *Essay on Motion* (1721), which challenged Isaac Newton's *Mathematical Principles of Natural Philosophy* (1687) by rejecting the notion that gravity was something fixed and "real" beyond what was observed through the senses. In turn, any motion in which there was no change between an object and the body that sensed it was also meaningless, ideas that some have claimed anticipated Einstein's theory of relatively.[46] Once again, underpinning Berkeley's thesis was his doctrine of immaterialism.

Headstrong in his beliefs and surely inspired by his American surroundings, Berkeley imbued his newest work with both his hard-won experience and penchant for literary experimentation. Once again employing Platonic dialogues, *Alciphron* advanced Berkeley's doctrine of immaterialism while criticizing the way "free thinkers" reduced nature to assemblages of mechanized parts. These were arguments he had polished over decades and a rhetorical methodology that had earned *Three Dialogues* acclaim. But in *Alciphron* Berkeley placed new emphasis on physical setting to illustrate his ideas.[47] If the Scientific Revolution had produced two competing conceptions of nature—one mechanical and another spiritual—then he would illustrate them using scenes from the world around him. As eighteenth-century literary scholar Tim Fulford has argued, "[L]andscape-description was . . . a means of making interventions in current political debates." A landscape, he continued, "constituted a place in which ideologies were proposed and contested."[48] For instance, Swift's dung-strewn Dublin evoked an "excremental vision" of eighteenth-century Irish politics; his stone-walled countryside conveyed the psychological confinement of political oppression.[49] Similarly, Berkeley, who according to legend spent countless hours contemplating the contents of *Alciphron* at the beach near his farm, staged his debates concerning God and science along the shores of Rhode Island Sound.

That the term "nature" was subject to such broad interpretation and wide application during the seventeenth and eighteenth centuries made it a particularly useful metaphor for describing the complexities of contemporary culture. As evidenced by some of the most celebrated early modern poetry and prose, natural features—and specifically rivers and coasts—often served as metaphors of social change. Widely considered the first English landscape poem, Sir John Denham's

"Cooper's Hill," (1641), described the Thames River near London. But instead of using analogies to convey philosophical or political ideas, Denham crafted landscape descriptions that evoked those tensions tacitly.[50] Writing amidst the turmoil faced by Charles I and his Long Parliament, Denham described the Thames as a powerful but benevolent monarch that flowed with "gentle Calmness" through the "steep horrid Roughness of the Wood." When the "rough" populace lived in harmony with the sovereign, or when "such huge Extreams [of] Nature doth unite," Denham explained, "Wonder from thence results, [and] from thence Delight."[51] But, Denham showed, if kings tried "grasping more than they could hold," they made their "Subjects by Oppression bold." And if, conversely, the people overreached, an equally rash response from the sovereign could be expected:

> But if with Bays and Dams, they strive to force
> His Chanel [sic] to a new or narrow Course;
> No longer then within his Banks he dwells,
> First to a Torrent, then a Deluge swells:
> Stronger and Fiercer! By Restraint he roars,
> And knows no Bound, but makes his Powers his Shores.[52]

The Thames River estuary near London was a place in which the "Extreams" of nature, land and sea, or the people and the Crown, overlapped. If the people attempted to alter the King's course, if they tinkered with the traditional channels of power, then environmental—read political—destruction would lead to catastrophe.

Denham's innovative use of littoral metaphor made a strong impression on some of the eighteenth century's most notable writers. Berkeley's friend and colleague Alexander Pope was particularly taken by Denham's ability to imbue physical forms with moral meaning. "The Descriptions of Places, and Images rais'd by the Poet," observed Pope of Denham, "are still tending to some Hint, or leading into some Reflection, upon moral Life or political Institution: Much in the same manner as the real Sight of such Scenes and Prospects is apt to give the Mind a compos'd Turn and incline it to Thoughts and Contemplations that have a Relation to the Object."[53] Following Denham's design, Pope penned his famous *Windsor-Forest* to celebrate limited monarchy, and in later drafts, the 1713 Treaty of Utrecht.[54] Specifically, Pope used the landscape to convey what he believed was a British rebirth under Queen Anne. In Windsor Forest, a politically stable Eden "vanished now so long," reappeared in such a way that "hills and vales, the woodland and the plain, . . . and earth and water" had reached accord. Among the headwaters of British liberty at Windsor, peace and prosperity coalesced, rolled into the estuary, and ebbed into the ocean. "[The] Unbounded *Thames*," he wrote, "shall flow for all mankind." To the "distant ends" of Europe and the Atlantic world, "our glory shall behold."[55] Pope's ability to raise "inexplicable beauties . . . so surprisingly, and at the same time so naturally out of a trifle," so impressed Berkeley that, after having read "The Rape of the Lock," he penned a letter to his friend, explaining, "I am charmed with the magic of your invention."[56]

Writing at about the same time, Berkeley's friend Joseph Addison used physical geography to advocate for social reform. Addison's "Pleasures of the Imagination," which he published in 1712 as a series of essays in *The Spectator* (which he co-edited with Richard Steele), used contrasting landscapes to convey the concept of social mobility to the magazine's largely middle-class audience. Addison depicted vast open spaces such as broad coastal meadows and the ocean to convey the growing breadth of possibility for the upwardly mobile. He consciously juxtaposed vertical features such as mountains and "high Rocks and Precipices," widely considered aristocratic geographies among contemporaries, with bourgeois deserts and broad bodies of water, in ways that assigned them equal importance.[57] Addison also used the interplay between land and water to illustrate changing conceptions of class. All things that splashed, shimmered, and flowed represented social dynamism, whereas the permanence of land symbolized the status quo. "[T]here is nothing that enlivens a Prospect," he wrote, "than Rivers, Jetteaus, or Falls of Water, where the Scene is perpetually shifting, and entertaining the Sight every Moment with something that is new. We are quickly tired," he continued, "with looking upon Hills and Valleys, where every thing continues fixed and settled in the same Place and Posture."[58] For Addison, the rushing waters of the middle class revealed opportunity and independence; the dusty immutability of mountains evoked the old order.

Strongly influenced by his close reading of and association with Addison, Steele, Swift, and Pope, Berkeley used Aquidneck Island and its beaches to frame his arguments concerning nature and theology. Structured around seven dialogues, *Alciphron* followed a small cast of characters as they debated the meaning of nature along the shores of Rhode Island Sound and Narragansett Bay. Berkeley advanced his own orthodox worldview through the characters Euphranor, a simple but well-read farmer, and Crito, a local pastor. The outspoken Alciphron and his impetuous companion Lysicles voiced the arguments of anti-Christian "free thinkers." The dialogues pitted a divinely inspired world against the "Minute Philosophers," or the theoretically diminutive "sect" that was content to reduce all "Human Nature . . . to the narrow low Standard of Animal Life."[59] Although the axes of eighteenth-century intellectual debate were never so square, Berkeley nevertheless narrated a powerful polarity developing between material existence and the divine, between "Animal Life" and "Immortality." In consequence, the careful, deliberate stylist juxtaposed improvement with Providence along the ocean's edge.[60] Just as Addison had paired the open spaces of opportunity with the promontories of patriarchy, Berkeley contrasted human progress ashore with eternity at sea.

But like any undulating coastline, the spaces where conceptions of nature collided were neither neat nor tidy. When Alciphron suggested early in the first dialogue that "minute philosopher" was not a term of derision but, rather, an appellation conveying "distinguished Perspicacity," Berkeley balked. Through Euphranor, he called minute philosophers "Pirates, who plunder all that come in their way." Those deist and atheist marauders who would deny a God-given reality sought only sensuality and, in turn, personal gain. So jarring was this way of seeing the world for Euphranor that the opinions of these skeptics made him feel "stript and desolate on a bleak Beach."[61] A world lacking God's direct intervention, the orthodox partisan avowed, left him naked and alone, doomed to wander a sandy purgatory somewhere between paradise and oblivion. Much like the indecisive doctrines of deism, which glorified God but did not want him around, the littoral margin was muddled and dispirited.

Far from the metaphorical turmoil of the beach, Berkeley's first dialogue opened with a scene of earthly Elysium among the farms and forests surrounding Whitehall. Alciphron, Lysicles, and Euphranor passed "through half a dozen pleasant Fields planted round with Plane-trees, that are very common in this part of the Country." After walking through the "delicious shade" of the forest, they arrived at Crito's house, which stood "in the middle of a small Park, beautify'd with two fine Groves of Oak and Walnut, and a winding Stream of sweet and clear water." In their initial exchange, the four admired "the Beauty of this rural Scene, the fine Season of the Year, and some late Improvements which had been made in the adjacent Country by new Methods of Agriculture."[62] Aquidneck Island, they all attested, had been improved by the efforts of man. Alciphron pushed the point further when he asserted that "It is to the noble Asserters of the Privilege and Perfection of Human kind, the Freethinkers I mean, who have sprung up and multiplied of late Years, that we are indebted for all those important Discoveries."[63] It was the promoters of scientific progress, in other words, who had advanced the agricultural arts and made the world a better place in the process.

For Alciphron, the human penchant for improvement extended well beyond the fields. "[T]he Mind of Man," he told his interlocutors, "may be fitly compared to a piece of Land. What stubbing, plowing, digging, and harrowing, is to the one; that thinking, reflecting, examining, is to the other." Refinement was an intellectual endeavor as well, and one, moreover, that was hindered by religion. Upon the land and within the mind, progress, he asserted, could only be cultivated when sheltered from "the Winds of Doctrine . . . , the Superstition of Fools, or the Imposture of Priests." Alciphron the atheist believed that mankind could only spark the fire of human initiative once he had turned his back to the gales of faith. Euphranor, conversely, believed it was divine favor that fanned spiritual development and brought order to all of nature. The "visible and natural World," he explained, was a unified system, defined by "mutual Connection and the Correspondence of Parts." This sense of "Perfection" and "Order" imbued nature with beauty. Similarly, he continued, one must "infer the same Union, Order, and Regularity in the moral World that we perceive to be in the natural." Therefore, he concluded, "the Belief of a God, of a future State, and of moral Duties are the only wise, right, and genuine Principles of Human Conduct."[64] In short, God brought harmony to nature and society. Faith was fundamental to human betterment. Among the manicured fields of Crito's farm, Berkeley had framed two very different conceptions of nature, at the heart of which were two competing interpretations of progress.

The first felt that intellectual and technological potential were stifled by religion. The second contended that God and faith in his ways was necessary for all forms of earthly prosperity.

So deeply divided were "freethinking" and orthodox conceptions of progress, so radically different were their ideas about the natural world, that Berkeley, imbuing place with purpose, evoked the coast for contrast. The following morning, the discussants walked to a nearby beach and ambled over "the smooth sand," of the intertidal, "with the Ocean on one hand, and on the other wild broken Rocks, intermixed with shady Trees and Springs of Water." As the sun climbed high in the sky, they "withdrew into a hollow Glade" and sat between two rocks, where they resumed their discussion at what was most likely Sachuest Beach, only a short distance from Berkeley's home. With the sound of the surf surely pounding before them, Eurphranor, and the "Minute Philosophers" Alciphron and Lycicles debated the ways that vice and virtue shaped the path to improvement. Euphranor claimed that "Vice is pernicious to the Public," and only the "Fear of God, and the Sense of a future State," would prevent men from degeneracy. Of his freethinking "sect," explained Lysicles, "We make Men relish the World, attentive to their Interests, lively and luxurious in their Pleasures, without Fear or Restraint from God or Man."[65]

Berkeley's discussion of vice was an outright attack on Bernard Mandeville's *Fable of the Bees*, which described a hive upon which virtuosity had been imposed by some external power (such as organized religion). When the bees "improv'd their Temperance," and learned "to avoid Extravagance," Mandeville quipped, their community failed, and those "Blest with Content and Honesty" simply flew off to live in a "hollow Tree." Ultimately, Mandeville argued that "Bare Virtue can't make Nations live/ In Splendor."[66] For Berkeley, who believed that inhibition reflected godliness, the suggestion that vice advanced the common good was maddening. An exasperated Crito admonished the minute philosophers for believing that happiness "consists of obeying Animal Instincts, Appetites, and Passions." If one denied man's capacity for restraint, then man was nothing more than "a Machine actuated according to the Laws of Motion," and his soul was "corporeal and dissolveth like a Flame or Vapour."[67] The champions of vice tied progress to self-interest and worldly pleasures. The partisans of restraint saw progress in the promise of everlasting life. Although the contrasts between "freethinking" and religion were rarely so sharp, the setting "on the Strand," between two ways of knowing nature, reflected what Berkeley believed were two overlapping but nevertheless contrasting conceptions of the cosmos.[68]

For one of Berkeley's most incendiary critics, nature was completely divorced from the divine. In his three-volume *Characteristics of Men, Manners, Opinions, Times* (1711), Anthony Ashley Cooper, the third Earl of Shaftesbury, claimed that nature had come first, and God was most likely conjured later in the minds of men. "O mighty Nature!" Shaftesbury exclaimed. "Wise substitute of Providence! impower'd Creatress! . . . Thee I invoke, and Thee alone adore."[69] So "boundless, unsearchable, [and] impenetrable," was Shaftesbury's agnostic notion of nature, that he likened it to an Ocean with "no Coast nor Limit" in sight. When he "sally'd forth into the wide *Expanse*," he returned humbled by its immensity so much that he "dare no more behold the amazing Depths, nor sound the Abyss of Deity."[70] If Berkeley's coast conveyed God's enduring presence, Shaftesbury's edgeless, bottomless sea depicted nature as all-consuming chaos, an alternative infinite spirit from which all virtue and beauty derived.

The suggestion that nature was somehow independent of God's plan (or that it was a deity in its own right) and that virtue could be achieved without organized religion and its prescribed boundaries enraged Berkeley. In *Alciphron*'s third dialogue he attacked Shaftesbury directly. Berkeley argued that "When a Man is conscious that his Will is inwardly conformed to the Divine Will, producing Order and Harmony in the Universe, and conducting the whole by the justest Methods to the best End: This gives a beautiful idea."[71] The crucible of Christianity, Berkeley believed, produced such moral purity that when its lid was lifted beauty radiated from the bowl. Contrary to Shaftesbury's claim that morality and, by extension, beauty was inherent in mankind and the material world, Berkeley argued that God was the sole source of earthly splendor. "I would fain know," he argued through Euphranor, "what beauty can be found in a moral system, formed, connected, and governed by chance, fate, or any other blind unthinking principle."[72] Without a constant divine presence, in other words, beauty, balance, and proportion could not exist.

As Berkeley and the sages with whom his work conversed soon realized, any attempt to define something so unwieldy and obscure as "nature" forced one to consider almost every aspect of human culture. *Alciphron* meandered from virtue to language, from grace to aesthetics, and from education to numerous other topics and back again. Taking pains to frame his claims along the edge of the sea, Berkeley structured his narrative to reflect the cyclical rhythms of the tide and imbued his arguments with the rhetorical powers of the littoral landscape. In his fifth dialogue, the discussants passed through a corridor of ornamental trees, to a "small Mount of Easy Ascent," at the top of which they sat under a "spreading Tree." From the summit of what was likely Honeyman's Hill near Whitehall, "on one Hand," they saw "a narrow Bay or Creek of the Sea, inclosed on either Side by a Coast beautified with Rocks and Woods, and green Banks and Farm-houses. At the End of the Bay was a small Town placed upon the Slope of a Hill, which from the Advantage of its Situation made a considerable Figure." Asserting his authority form a position of elevation, Berkeley described the town of Newport and the view across Narragansett Bay, musing that "Several Fishing-boats and Lighters gliding up and down on a Surface as smooth and bright as Glass enlivened the Prospect."[73] When they looked down the hill "On the other hand," they saw "green Pastures, Flocks, and Herds, basking beneath in Sun-shine." So inspiring was the union of these two vistas that "here," wrote Berkeley, "we felt that sort of joyful Instinct which a rural Scene and fine Weather inspire." There they sat "resuming and continuing our Conference without Interruption till Dinner."[74] Among the distant shores of the empire, where earthly and divine realities could be surveyed in all their entirety and serenity, Berkeley balanced ocean and inland, town and country, upland and lowland, rock and wood, light and shade, placidity and movement. Here was the "Order and Harmony in the Universe" that God created.

BROKEN CISTERNS

By the summer of 1731 when he completed the manuscript for *Alciphron*, Berkeley knew that St. Paul's would never be. He had waited months for funds to arrive to no avail. The interminable nature of reality—even if it was only a perception—bore down on him. The whole plan, he wrote in *Alciphron*'s introduction, had been a "miscarriage," and his book an opportunity to "make . . . amends."[75] Shortly after baptizing his newborn daughter, Lucia, she died in early September. Saddled with despair, Berkeley packed his family's bags, donated his house, farm, and "every of their appurtenances" to Yale, stipulating that any income from the property be used to fund graduate study in divinity.[76] Still determined to realize his educational dreams in America, Berkeley had books shipped from London to Harvard and a collection of about 1,000 volumes to Yale, which in 1742 was estimated to be one third of its total.[77] As a sign of gratitude, Yale's Divinity School later adopted Berkeley's name, and in 1873 so too did the first branch of the University of California.[78]

After returning to London, Berkeley published *Alciphron* in 1732. The frontispiece of the first edition depicted a small cataract flowing into a cracked man-made catchment, which spilled its water on the ground.[79] The image was accompanied by a passage from the Book of Jeremiah (2:13): "They have forsaken me the Fountain of living waters, and hewed them out cisterns, broken cisterns that can hold no water."[80] Worshipping the false idols of progress, mankind had abandoned God's eternal spring for the stagnate pools of the material world. When those earthly creations crumbled and the water ran dry, man could either perish or return to Nature's one true author.

Berkeley rendered the land and waterscapes of southern Rhode Island into powerful symbols. His ideas showcase the complex ways in which piety and progress, empiricism and rationalism communicated during the age of Enlightenment.[81] Where the material world met the immaterial and "freethinking" merged with orthodoxy, nature and culture became inextricably entangled. In small ways, Berkeley had begun to construct a moral geography for a hybrid world.

Indirectly, these ideas came to shape the ways people imagined and interacted with nature. Following the publication of William Cronon's now famous essay "The Trouble with Wilderness," environmental activists and a number of prominent historians, including Samuel Hays, criticized Cronon for defining wilderness as a "world of abstracted ideas." Hays feared that Cronon had denied the importance of protecting material nature, which could potentially "divert" environmentalists away from meaningful action and instead into the intellectual "thickets."[82]

ALCIPHRON:

OR, THE
MINUTE PHILOSOPHER.
IN
SEVEN DIALOGUES.

Containing an APOLOGY *for the* Christian Religion,
against those who are called Free-thinkers.

VOLUME *the* FIRST.

They have forsaken me the Fountain of living waters, and hewed them
out cisterns, broken cisterns that can hold no water. Jerem. ii. 13.
Sin mortuus, ut quidam minuti Philosophi censent, nihil sentiam,
non vereor ne hunc errorem meum mortui Philosophi irrideant.
Cicero.

LONDON:
Printed for J. TONSON in the *Strand,* 1732.

By Bishop Berkeley

Figure 2. The frontispiece to George Berkeley's first edition of *Alciphron*.

Cronon had intended to show that America's preoccupation with preserving wilderness had perhaps blinded some to environmental problems closer to home. Cultural notions of nature, in other words, shaped the way people chose to either protect or neglect it. One of his most outspoken critics, Bill Willers, felt that reducing nature to a set of cultural values denied its role as an "indispensible aspect of organic evolution."[83] Nature as an idea met nature as matter—the same quandary with which Berkeley had grappled more than 250 years earlier.

The impasse provided two simple narratives. Cronon's essay ended with a message of renewal. The careful consideration of and "deep reflection" upon nature as an idea, Cronon explained, "means looking at the part of nature we intend to turn toward our own ends and asking whether we can use it again and again and again."[84] Willers, conversely, feared that overlooking the materiality of wilderness could push wild nature down the slippery slope toward catastrophic decline. But perhaps there is room for compromise, and one that carries with it the imprimatur of time. For in a world where no corner of the globe has been left untouched, we must come to recognize, as Berkeley did from atop Honeyman's Hill, that within the dialectical relationship between matter and human ideas, between the "natural" and the cultural, there exists a sense of balance, proportion, and beauty all its own. An environmental ethic for a hybrid world might even begin to mend the rift between what Paul Sabin has described as the "incompatible viewpoints" of those who demand environmental restraint and those who seek unfettered economic growth.[85]

Although the impassioned pleas of an embattled philosopher were dismissed by many in his own time and have been forgotten by many in our own, Berkeley's ideas reveal that a hybrid world constitutes much more than the sum of its parts. Finding a place within that world requires moderation, devotion, reverence, scientific and poetic experimentation, and the recognition that all landscapes are suffused with meaning.

CHRISTOPHER PASTORE is assistant professor of history at the University at Albany, State University of New York. He is the author of *Between Land and Sea: The Atlantic Coast and the Transformation of New England* (2014).

NOTES

1. George Berkeley, Newport, R.I., to Thomas Prior, April 24, 1729, in *The Works of George Berkeley Bishop of Cloyne*, vol. 8, *Letters* eds. A. A. Luce and T. E. Jessop (London: Thomas Nelson and Sons Ltd., 1956), 196.

2. Edwin S. Gaustad, *George Berkeley in America* (New Haven, Conn: Yale University Press, 1979), 14; George Berkeley, Newport, R.I., to Thomas Prior, June 12, 1729, *The Works of George Berkeley*, vol. 8, 198.

3. George Berkeley, Newport, R.I., to Sir John Percival, March 29, 1730, *The Works of George Berkeley*, vol. 8, 205; George Berkeley, Newport, R.I., to Sir John Percival, February 7, 1728/1729, *The Works of George Berkeley*, vol. 8, 190–191; Edwin S. Gaustad, *George Berkeley in America*, 12–14; "London, October 8," *American Weekly Mercury* no. 474 (18 January to 4 February 1728–9): 3.

4. Mark Antony DeWolfe Howe, "Dwellers in Old Dwellings: George Berkeley at Whitehall and Adamses at Quincy," *Proceedings of the Massachusetts Historical Society* 70, 3rd Series (Oct., 1950–May, 1953): 21.

5. George Berkeley, Newport, R.I., to Sir John Percival, March 18, 1729, in *The Works of George Berkeley*, vol. 8, 191–192.

6. On commercial expansion in early eighteenth-century Newport, see Lynne Withey, *Urban Growth in Colonial Rhode Island: Newport and Providence in the Eighteenth Century* (Albany: State University of New York Press, 1984), 20; Carl Bridenbaugh, *Cities in the Wilderness: The First Century of Urban Life in America, 1625–1742* (New York: The Ronald Press Company, 1938), 362.

7. George Berkeley, London, to Sir John Percival, March 4, 1722/1723, in *The Works of George Berkeley*, vol. 8, 127–129.

8. Scott Breuninger, *Recovering Bishop Berkeley: Virtue and Society in the Anglo-Irish Context* (New York: Palgrave Macmillan, 2010), 100.

9. Gaustad, *George Berkeley in America*, 47–54; George Berkeley, Newport, R.I., to Henry Newman, June 27, 1729, in *The Works of George Berkeley*, vol. 8, 200.

10. George Berkeley, *A Proposal for the Better Supplying of Churches in our Foreign Plantations and for Converting the Savage Americans to Christianity by a College to be Erected in the Summer Islands, Otherwise Called the Isles of Bermuda* (1725) in *The Works of George Berkeley, D.D.: Formerly Bishop of Cloyne*, vol. 3, ed. Alexander Campbell Fraser, M.A. (Oxford: Clarendon Press, 1871), 229.

11. J. G. A. Pocock, *Barbarism and Religion: The Enlightenment of Edward Gibbon, 1737–1764* (Cambridge: Cambridge University Press, 1999), 5.

12. David Sorkin, *The Religious Enlightenment: Protestants, Jews, and Catholics from London to Vienna* (Princeton: Princeton University Press, 2008), 3.

13. Sarah Rivett, *The Science of the Soul in Colonial New England* (Chapel Hill: University of North Carolina Press, 2011), 9–12.

14. Roderick Nash's *Wilderness and the American Mind* (New Haven, Conn.: Yale University Press, 1967) did much to connect environmental history to the history of ideas. Richard White identified the ways the wilderness "idea" narrative developed alongside the material change narrative in "American Environmental History: The Development of a New Historical Field," *Pacific Historical Review* 54, no. 3 (August 1985): 297–335. The debates between "material" nature and ideas about nature were best exemplified in an exchange between Donald Worster and William Cronon

in Donald Worster "Transformations of the Earth: Toward an Agroecological Perspective in History," *Journal of American History*, 76 (March 1990): 1087–1106 and William Cronon, "Modes of Prophecy and Production: Placing Nature in History," Ibid.: 1122–31. Also see William Cronon, ed., *Uncommon Ground: Rethinking the Human Place in Nature* (New York: Norton, 1995). Following William Cronon's *Changes in the Land: Indians, Colonists, and the Ecology of New England* (New York: Hill and Wang, 1983) there have been innumerable environmental histories that focus on the changing material world and its importance to human history. In the book's twentieth anniversary addition, Cronon admitted that the book was "relentlessly materialistic," which he attributed to the book's "virtual silence on matters pertaining to religion" (p. 184). Since environmental history has gained momentum as a field, there have been fewer studies on the history of environmental ideas. Nevertheless, important works include Carolyn Merchant, *The Death of Nature: Women, Ecology, and the Scientific Revolution* (New York: Harper and Row, 1980) and Neil Evernden, *The Social Creation of Nature* (Baltimore: The Johns Hopkins University Press, 1992). Donald Worster traced the evolution of ecological ideas in *Nature's Economy: A History of Ecological Ideas* (New York: Cambridge, 1994). And Richard Judd has argued that these early forms of ecological thought sowed the seeds of an American conservation ethic in *The Untilled Garden: Natural History and the Origins of American Conservation, 1730–1850* (New York: Cambridge University Press, 2009).

15. Paul S. Sutter, "The World With Us: The State of American Environmental History," *Journal of American History* 100, no. 1 (June 2013): 96; See also Richard White, "From Wilderness to Hybrid Landscapes: The Cultural Turn in Environmental History," *Historian* 66 (Fall 2004): 557–64.

16. See Keith Thomas, *Man and the Natural World: A History of the Modern Sensibility* (New York: Pantheon Books, 1983). Thomas argues that it was during the early modern period that "there occurred a whole cluster of changes in the way in which men and women, at all social levels, perceived and classified the natural world around them" (p. 15). See also John F. Richards, *The Unending Frontier: An Environmental History of the Early Modern World* (Berkeley: University of California Press, 2006) and Clarence J. Glacken, *Traces on the Rhodian Shore: Nature and Culture in Western Thought from Ancient Times to the End of the Eighteenth Century* (Berkeley: University of California Press, 1976). On the Scottish Enlightenment and its impact on environmental thought see, Frederick Albritton Jonsson, *Enlightenment's Frontier: The Scottish Highlands and the Origins of Environmentalism* (New Haven, Conn.: Yale University Press, 2013). On early modern islands and the origins of environmentalism, see Richard Grove, *Green Imperialism: Colonial Expansion, Tropical Island Edens and the Origins of Environmentalism, 1600–1860* (New York: Cambridge University Press, 1996) and John Gillis, *iu* (New York: Palgrave Macmillan, 2004). On early modern coastal environments and changing environmental thought, see Christopher L. Pastore, *Between Land and Sea: The Atlantic Coast and the Transformation of New England* (Cambridge, Mass.: Harvard University Press, 2014) and John Gillis, *The Human Shore: Seacoasts in History* (Chicago: Chicago University Press, 2012). On changing conceptions of early modern climate, see Jan Golinski *British Weather and the Climate of Enlightenment*

(Chicago: University of Chicago Press, 2007); Vladimir Janković, *Reading the Skies: A Cultural History of English Weather, 1650–1820* (Chicago: University of Chicago Press, 2000); Matthew Mulcahy, *Hurricanes and Society in the British Greater Caribbean, 1624–1783* (Baltimore: Johns Hopkins University Press, 2008); James Delbourgo, *A Most Amazing Scene of Wonders: Electricity and Enlightenment in Early America* (Cambridge, Mass.: Harvard University Press, 2006). For an overview of early modern science in imperial contexts, see James Delbourgo and Nicholas Dew, *Science and Empire in the Atlantic World* (New York: Routledge, 2008) and Richard Drayton, *Nature's Government: Science, Imperial Britain, and the "Improvement" of the World* (New Haven, Conn.: Yale University Press, 2000); On natural history, see Susan Scott Parish, *American Curiosity: Cultures of Natural History in the Colonial British Atlantic World* (Chapel Hill: University of North Carolina Press, 2006); Londa Schiebinger, *Plants and Empire: Colonial Bioprospecting in the Atlantic World* (Cambridge, Mass.: Harvard University Press, 2007); and Richard Judd, *The Untilled Garden: Natural History and the Spirit of Conservation in America, 1740–1840* (New York: Cambridge University Press, 2009).

17. Paul S. Sutter, "The World With Us," 97.

18. Simon Schama, *Landscape & Memory* (London: Harper Collins, 1995), 9–10. Schama argues that "landscapes that we suppose to be most free of our culture may turn out, on closer inspection, to be its product." It is, he explains "our shaping perception that makes the difference between raw matter and landscape."

19. Richard C. Vitzthum, *Materialism: An Affirmative History and Definition* (Amherst, N.Y.: Prometheus Books, 1995), 64.

20. Evan Berry, *Devoted to Nature: The Religious Roots of American Environmentalism* (Berkeley: University of California Press, 2015). Focusing largely on the nineteenth century, Berry has identified in American environmentalism a "historically demonstrable genealogical affinity with Christian theological tradition," p. 2. Similarly, in his study of the genesis of conservation ideas in America, Richard Judd has shown that Cotton Mather's inquiries into natural history were suffused with religious ideas. See Judd, *The Untilled Garden*, 23–28. These arguments challenge that of Lynn White Jr., who argued that Christianity caused environmental decline. See Lynn White Jr., "The Historical Roots of Our Ecologic Crisis," *Science* 155, no. 3767 (March 10, 1967): 1203–1207.

21. Breuninger, *Recovering Bishop Berkeley*, 4.

22. Steven Mentz, "Maritime Culture and Early Modern English Literature," *Literature Compass* 6, no. 5 (2009): 1001, 1008.

23. George Berkeley, Newport, to Sir John Percival, March 4, 1728/1729, in *The Works of George Berkeley*, vol. 8, 127.

24. George Berkeley, Newport, to Sir John Percival, February 7, 1728/1729, in *The Works of George Berkeley*, vol. 8, 190.

25. A. A. Luce, *The Life of George Berkeley: Bishop of Cloyne* (London: Thomas Nelson and Sons, Ltd., 1949), 123; George Berkeley, Newport, R.I., to Bishop Benson, April 11, 1729, in *The Works of George Berkeley*, vol. 8, 193–194.

26. George Berkeley, Newport, R.I., to Thomas Prior, April 24, 1729, in *The Works of George Berkeley*, vol. 8, 196.

27. Gaustad, *George Berkeley in America*, 82; Mark Antony DeWolfe Howe, "Dwellers in Old Dwellings," 25.

28. Personal tour of Whitehall with Professor Timo Airaksinen of the University of Helsinki. August 29, 2012.

29. A. A. Luce, *The Life of George Berkeley*, 123; Also see Stephen Saunders Webb, "The Strange Career of Francis Nicholson," *William and Mary Quarterly* 23, no. 4 (1966): 520. Webb explained, "Next to the army, the church was royalism's strongest bulwark.... [T]he Church had a power over men's minds probably a good deal greater than that the army had over their bodies."

30. George Berkeley, Newport, R.I., to Thomas Prior, June 12, 1729, in *The Works of George Berkeley*, vol. 8, 198.

31. George Berkeley, Newport, to Sir John Percival, August 30, 1729, in *The Works of George Berkeley*, vol. 8, 202.

32. "Boston, Jan. 22," *Boston News-Letter*, January 15–22, 1730, 2.

33. George Berkeley, Newport, R.I., to Sir John Percival, March 29, 1730, in *The Works of George Berkeley*, vol. 8, 205.

34. George Berkeley, *Alciphron; Or the Minute Philosopher. In Seven Dialogues Containing an Apology for the Christian Religion, against those who are called Free-Thinkers* (London: J. and R. Tonson and S. Draper, 1752), 2.

35. A. A. Luce, *The Life of George Berkeley: Bishop of Cloyne* (London: Thomas Nelson and Sons, Ltd., 1949), 21–26.

36. Ibid., 29–32.

37. Ibid., 41–42.

38. George Berkeley, *Principles of Human Knowledge and Three Dialogues*, ed. Roger Woolhouse (New York: Penguin, 2004), 6–9.

39. Robert Boyle, *Free Inquiry into the Vulgarly Received Notion of Nature*, eds. Edward B. Davis and Michael Hunter (New York: Cambridge University Press, 1996), 13.

40. George Berkeley, *Principals of Human Knowledge and Three Dialogues*, 64.

41. Sir John Percival, London, to George Berkeley, August 26, 1710, in *The Correspondence of George Berkeley Afterwards Bishop of Cloyne and Sir John Percival Afterward Earl of Egmont*, ed. Benjamin Rand (Cambridge: Cambridge University Press, 1914), 80–81; Gausted, *George Berkeley in America*, 57.

42. Sir John Percival, London, to George Berkeley, October 30, 1710, in *The Correspondence of George Berkeley and John Percival*, 87; A. A. Luce, *The Life of George Berkeley*, 51.

43. A. A. Luce, *The Life of George Berkeley*, 57.

44. George Berkeley, London, to Sir John Percival, March 27, 1712/1713, in *The Correspondence of George Berkeley and John Percival*, 111–112.

45. A. A. Luce, *The Life of George Berkeley*, 69.

46. W. A. Suchting, "Berkeley's Criticism of Newton on Space and Motion," *Isis* 58, no. 2 (Summer, 1967): 187; Desmond M. Clarke, ed., *Berkeley: Philosophical Writing* (New York: Cambridge University Press, 2008), xxiv–xxv.

47. Peter Walmsley, *The Rhetoric of Berkeley's Philosophy* (Cambridge, U.K.: Cambridge University Press, 1990), 66–67.

48. Tim Fulford, *Landscape, Liberty and Authority: Poetry, Criticism and Politics from Thomson to Wordsworth* (New York: Cambridge University Press, 1996), 5–6.

49. Carole Fabricant, *Swift's Landscape* (Notre Dame, Ind.: University of Notre Dame Press, 1995), 24–42, 43–54.

50. John T. Ogden, "From Spatial to Aesthetic Distance in the Eighteenth Century," *Journal of the History of Ideas* 35, no. 1 (Jan.-Mar., 1974): 68. Theodore H. Banks, "Sir John Denham's 'Cooper's Hill,'" *The Modern Language Review* 21, No. 3 (Jul., 1926): 269, argued that Denham's landscape descriptions were "relatively unimportant, being to a large extent conventional or vaguely general, and serving merely as a peg on which to hang ethical and philosophical reflections." Rufus Putney, however, argued in "The View from Cooper's Hill," *University of Colorado Studies in Language and Literature* vol. 6 (1957): 13–22, that Denham's use of landscape to convey political meaning was quite innovative.

51. Sir John Denham, *Cooper's Hill* (London: H. Hills, 1709), 12.

52. Ibid., 16.

53. Maynard Mack, ed., *The Poems of Alexander Pope,* vol. 8 (New Haven, Conn.: Yale University Press, 1967), n. 466 to *Illiad* XVI, quoted in John T. Ogden, "From Spatial to Aesthetic Distance in the Eighteenth Century," 68.

54. Vincent Carretta, "Anne and Elizabeth: The Poet as Historian in Windsor Forest" *Studies in English Literature, 1500–1900* 21, no. 3, *Restoration and Eighteenth Century* (Summer, 1981): 425–437.

55. Alexander Pope, "Windsor-Forest," in *Miscellaneous Poems and Translations by Several Hands* (London: Bernard Linton, 1720), 7, 24.

56. George Berkeley, Leghorn, to Alexander Pope, May 1, 1714 in *The Works of George Berkeley,* vol. 8, 82–83.

57. Carole Fabricant, "The Aesthetics and Politics of Landscape in the Eighteenth Century," in *Studies in Eighteenth-Century British Art and Aesthetics,* ed. Ralph Cohen (Berkeley: University of California Press, 1985), 54–55.

58. Joseph Addison, *The Spectator III,* as discussed in Fabricant, "The Aesthetics and Politics of Landscape in the Eighteenth Century," 59.

59. George Berkeley, *Alciphron,* 23.

60. On Berkeley as a literary stylist, see Bonamy Dobrée, "Berkeley as a Man of Letters," *Hermathena* 82 (Nov. 1953): 49–75.

61. George Berkeley, *Alciphron,* 23.

62. Ibid., 5.

63. Ibid., 6.

64. Ibid., 6–7, 44.

65. Ibid., 47, 71.

66. Bernard Mandeville, *The Fable of the Bee or, Private Vices, Publick Benefits* (London: T. Johnson, 1724), 22, 24.

67. George Berkeley, *Alciphron,* 100.

68. Ibid., 105.

69. Anthony Ashley Cooper, the third Earl of Shaftesbury, *Characteristicks: An Inquiry Concerning Virtue and Merit. The Moralist; a Philosophical Rhapsody* vol. 2 (London: 1733), 345.

70. Ibid., 345–346.

71. George Berkeley, *Alciphron,* 129.

72. Ibid., 127.

73. George Berkeley, *Alciphron*, 187; On landscape and elevation, see Tim Fulford, *Landscape, Liberty and Authority*, 11.
74. George Berkeley, *Alciphron*, 187.
75. Ibid., 2.
76. Gaustad, *George Berkeley in America*, 161, 84; A. A. Luce, *The Life of George Berkeley*, 236–237.
77. Gaustad, *George Berkeley in America*, 86.
78. Ibid., 197, 201.
79. David Berman, "Bishop Berkeley and the Fountains of Living Water," *Hermathena* 128 (1980): 21–31.
80. George Berkeley, *Alciphron: Or, the Minute Philosopher. In Seven Dialogues Containing an Apology for the Christian Religion, against those who are called Free-Thinkers* (London: J. Tonson, 1732).
81. Paul Russell, "Causation, Cosmology, and the Limits of Philosophy: The Early Eighteenth-Century British Debate," in *The Oxford Handbook of British Philosophy in the Eighteenth Century*, ed. James A. Harris. Oxford, U.K.: Oxford University Press, 2013), 615–620.
82. William Cronon, "The Trouble with Wilderness; or, Getting Back to the Wrong Nature," in *Uncommon Ground: Rethinking the Human Place in Nature*, ed. William Cronon (New York: Norton, 1996), 69–90; Samuel P. Hays, "The Trouble with Bill Cronon's Wilderness," *Environmental History* 1, no. 1 (January 1996): 31–32.
83. Bill Willers, "The Trouble with Cronon," *Wild Earth* 59 (Winter 1996/1997): 59–61.
84. Cronon, "The Trouble with Wilderness," 89.
85. Paul Sabin, *The Bet: Paul Ehrlich, Julian Simon, and Our Gamble over Earth's Future* (New Haven, Conn.: Yale University Press, 2013), 217.

Everyday Modernities

J. B. Jackson and the Postwar American Landscape

JEFFREY D. BLANKENSHIP

Abstract

In his writing in Landscape *magazine, the essayist and critic John Brinckerhoff Jackson (1909–1996) championed a focus on the "everyday" mid-century American landscape. My argument in this paper is that Jackson's writing has enduring relevance for understanding the relationship of modernity to everyday landscapes. Specifically, I develop the concept of "everyday modernities" in order to define and specify the lens through which Jackson sought to reconcile the logics of modernity with the lived realities of mid-century American life. Pulling this concept through two examples of his work—the "other-directedness" of landscape and the bodied landscapes of the hot-rodder—I show how Jackson endeavored to understand how these logics were embedded in some of the most common landscapes. He limned an approach to the modern landscape that took seriously the binary structure of modernist ideology (nature and culture, country and city), but strove to recognize the impacts of this ideology through the networks and connections that produce the material realities of everyday life. While Jackson's particular lens is certainly a very personal one, his interests and approach can help to reveal new connections and inspire new questions about the modern American landscape.*

INTRODUCTION

For well over sixty years, John Brinckerhoff Jackson (1909–1996) has been a familiar name to anyone interested in the study of American landscapes. Numerous scholars have written about him as the most eloquent proponent for understanding "common," "ordinary," or "everyday" landscapes.[1] Because most of Jackson's early essays were written during a period when modernist ideologies dominated discourses around the built environment, he is often portrayed as an enigmatic figure that found banal and mundane landscapes more interesting than the utopian proposals of mid-century visionaries. While this is largely true, it is important to note that his interests were not borne out of an anti-modern sentiment as much as a suspicion of utopian schemes that discounted the everyday experiences of ordinary people. For Jackson, the American landscape was a vibrantly complex reflection of modernity playing out in the material reality of everyday human environments.

Over the course of a 17-year period (1951–1968) as an essayist in *Landscape* (the magazine he founded and edited during this period), Jackson championed a focus on the everyday American landscape as a subject worthy of a level of critical scrutiny that paralleled the best social criticism of the day. In his essays and commentaries in *Landscape*, Jackson was concerned with how modernity was embedded in the most common landscapes. Jackson was writing within an intellectual milieu that had begun to question the role of elite tastemakers and cultural critics who privileged notions of "civilized" culture and high art over the expressions and experiences of everyday people. As a well-travelled, broadly educated, and widely read intellectual who shunned alignment with any particular discipline, Jackson wrote essays that were unusual in the mid-twentieth century for the expansive way they spoke of landscapes as artifacts of social and cultural processes.

My argument in this paper is that Jackson's writing in *Landscape* magazine has enduring relevance for understanding the relationship of modernity to everyday landscapes. Specifically, I develop the concept of "everyday modernities" in order to define and specify the lens through which Jackson sought to reconcile the logics of modernity with the everyday, lived realities of mid-century American life. This concept of everyday modernities, which I develop through the work of two contemporary scholars of modernity, James C. Scott and Bruno Latour, also helps to highlight the continued significance of Jackson's work. Through case studies of two provocative ideas within Jackson's writing—the "other-directedness" of landscape and the bodied, experiential landscape of the hot-rodder—I demonstrate how his approach to the modern landscape took seriously the binaries of modernist ideology (nature and culture, country and city), and yet sought to recognize the impacts of this ideology through the networks and connections that produce the material realities of everyday life.

To be sure, Jackson's approach to landscape was also personal—and quite eclectic; it was a product of his particular, and perhaps peculiar, life experiences. Jackson's biography reveals a life that fluidly moved between vastly different worlds. He was born in Dinard, France to wealthy American parents who placed him in some of the best private schools in Europe (Le Rosey) and America (Choate, Deerfield). Because of this cosmopolitan upbringing, he was comfortable navigating within elite social circles. After his parents divorced, however, he lived more modestly with his mother and spent his summers on his uncle's New Mexico ranch, where he was first introduced to the people and landscapes of the American Southwest.[2]

Jackson continued his education with a year in an experimental program at the University of Wisconsin, before transferring to Harvard, where he graduated in 1932 with a degree in history and literature. He also spent a year studying architecture at MIT and another year studying illustration in Vienna, before taking off on a two-year motorcycle journey across Europe. Jackson enlisted during World War II, but was quickly promoted to an intelligence officer due to his elite pedigree and fluency in French, German and Spanish. After the War, Jackson decided to return to the Southwest and settle into a life of ranching in New Mexico. He worked as a cowboy on a large ranch in northeastern New Mexico, and found that he loved his work. "[Jackson] reflected that he responded as he did to ranch life not because he was tolerant but because he had in him a streak of commonness."[3]

Unfortunately, but perhaps serendipitously, Jackson was thrown from a horse and spent a year recovering. During his convalescence, he began planning a magazine that would explore his adopted region of the Southwest. Initially finding inspiration in the methods of geographers who studied the landscape as an artifact of human culture, he founded *Landscape: The Human Geography of the Southwest* in 1951; however, within a year Jackson realized that the magazine's subject should not be limited to the region and changed the subtitle to *Magazine of Human Geography*. From the beginning, he self-published (and self-financed) his journal and was the sole author of its first issues.[4] Soon though, contributors and subscribers discovered the magazine and were attracted to Jackson's personal and editorial voice—a voice that had been shaped by 41 years of reading, travel and—most importantly—observation.

Although his early life was shaped by an elite upbringing, Jackson was drawn to the lives of working class and middle class American's who were finding their place in a rapidly changing world. It was toward an understanding of the daily realities of everyday Americans that Jackson would focus his writing in *Landscape*.

Most who have written about Jackson have done so via biographical reflections that paint him as an enigmatic but influential figure.[5] This is understandable; Jackson led an interesting and unique life, and his personal story is undoubtedly fascinating. Without discounting the importance of this scholarship, in this paper I seek to add to these historical reflections by attending to the aspects of his work that go beyond biography—that become useful and enduring techniques or approaches for the study of landscape. The most recent scholarly works to attempt to look beyond Jackson's biography are *Everyday America: Cultural Landscape Studies after J. B. Jackson*, edited by Chris Wilson and Paul Groth and *Drawn to Landscape: The Pioneering Work of J. B. Jackson*, edited by Janet Mendelsohn and Chris Wilson. Both are compilations of essays on Jackson's work and influence, and also windows into how the project of cultural landscape studies has been carried forward since Jackson. The authors who contribute to these volumes paint an image of Jackson as an influential figure who inspired others to observe the landscape culturally, to follow visual patterns and, most importantly, to ask questions.[6] Here I wish to extend the literature on Jackson's relevance by describing how his seemingly enigmatic approach was actually a useful lens for better understanding the mid-century landscape, as well as the modern landscapes of today.

THEORIZING EVERYDAY MODERNITIES

J. B. Jackson was an essayist and critic; he was not a theorist of modernity, at least not in the consistent and coherent way that is expected in the academy today. But his work nevertheless has important and enduring value for understanding the modern landscape. Jackson's writing, sometimes frustratingly, embodied the contradictions that he saw in the modern landscape. His work was both straight forward and counterintuitive, clear and cryptic, coherent and inconsistent. Rather than drawing definitive conclusions, Jackson focused his attention on lifting the (perhaps privileged) veil that prevented others from seeing modernity as it was—as embedded in and emergent from the everyday American landscape.[7] As the geographer Donald Meinig observed:

> Jackson points the way in his insistence on looking the modern scene squarely in the face; and his admonition is not simply for us to be comprehensive and tolerant, but to see the ordinary landscapes of the automobile, mobile home, supermarket, and shopping center as legitimately "vernacular"—that is, native to the area, but area now defined more at the national than the local scale.[8]

In this section, I want to elaborate on what I mean by everyday modernities, a term that I use to describe Jackson's contributions to the (modern) landscape idea—that is, to the study of landscape as a (modern) cultural concept.[9] Meinig's above praise of Jackson sheds some light on the dialectical nature of Jackson's work: his ability to see the overarching logics of modernity everywhere in mid-century America, while simultaneously insisting on understanding this modernity as creating an organization of "vernacular" spaces experienced by everyday people adjusting to new patterns across the national landscape. The term everyday modernities is meant to capture this dialectic, as it acknowledges modernity as a national (and global) set of forces, but recognizes that everyday life occurs within and reproduces these patterns.

The work of two scholars of modernity helps to build this concept more fully. The first is the work of political scientist James C. Scott on high-modernist ideology, which Scott defines as

> a strong, one might even say muscle-bound, version of the self-confidence about scientific and technical progress, the expansion of production, the growing satisfaction of human needs, the mastery of nature (including human nature), and, above all, the rational design of social order commensurate with the scientific understanding of natural laws.[10]

Scott explains that high-modernist ideology was often uncritically optimistic about the possibilities for comprehensive planning, and required state action to bring it into being, through plans, policies, and forms of social organization. In his book *Seeing Like a State*, Scott is particularly interested in some of the most devastating projects of state engineering that were influenced by high-modernist ideology (for example the unyielding rigidity of Le Corbusier's urban plans or the strict formality of German scientific forestry, ideas that spread around the world with often disastrous consequences). Indeed, he clarifies that his critique is particularly against "the imperialism of high-modernist, planned social order. . . . that excludes . . . local knowledge."[11] In other words, Scott was interested in exploring what happens when planning venerates the logics of modernity and ignores the particularities of the everyday.

Jackson would likely have agreed with Scott's critique; indeed, their projects are not incompatible. Nevertheless, whereas Scott focused on the imperialism of an ideology, Jackson is less scornful of the over-arching power structures that are generating modernity; instead he is more interested in the material realities of ordinary life in a modernizing world. It is useful to distinguish here between modernity and modernization. While modernity can be used to describe a dominant ideology, modernization describes the varied, material ways in which modernity comes into being. In other words, the term modernization signals the existence of something that we might understand as "actually existing modernities," as opposed to the (imagined) monolith *modernity*. This distinction extends from the work of scholars of neoliberalization, who point to the need to view neoliberal capitalism not as a uniform set of values and structures but rather as a diverse range of productions that are influenced by a dominant ideology but also particular to the land-scapes in which they emerge.[12] Similarly, actually existing *modernities* would point to the varied, everyday ways that modernization happens on the ground.

The second scholar whose work on modernity I find useful here is the science studies theorist Bruno Latour. Latour provocatively claims "we have never been modern."[13] In his book of the same title, Latour presents an ontological argument about (non)modernity that helps to deepen the concept of everyday modernities. To be truly modern, Latour argues, is to see and practice the world as a set of binaries: nature and culture, biology and society, human and nonhuman. These bina-ries, of course, underlie high-modernist ideology: the faith in humans' mastery of nature, and the certainty of scientific and technological progress. And yet, as Latour argues, these binaries don't actually exist. Instead, the modern project only exists through "the proliferation of hybrids down below."[14] That is, while (high-)modernist ideology attempts to separate the human and nonhuman world into distinct ontological zones (what Latour calls the work of purification), modernization exist only as a continually evolving set of networks, or hybrids—as nature-cultures, rather than distinct natures and cultures.[15] To be sure, these material realities are not exclusive of (high-)modernist ideology itself; indeed, the ideology is part of what informs and produces particular forms of modernization—sometimes with disastrous consequences, as Scott's work demonstrates. Nevertheless, what Latour's work points to is the importance of attending simultaneously to the processes of purification (the high-modernist ideology) and hybridization (the diverse realities of modernization).

The concept of everyday modernities takes seriously the "proliferation of hybrids," attending at once to the logics of (high-)modernity and to the varied ways that these logics emerge materially through the processes of everyday life. Of course, J. B. Jackson wrote about modernity decades before either Latour or Scott; and yet, while his terminology was different (and decidedly not academic), Jackson's work on the modern landscape in many ways anticipates both their work. Jackson wrote at a time in which there was great interest in "the everyday"—not (necessarily) as an antidote to the failed utopian planning schemes of high-modernist ideology,[16] but rather as the location where modernist thinking was taken up, produced, and transformed in the diverse processes of everyday life.[17] While pop artists pursued the subject of everyday modernity through the ironic display of consumer culture, and beat writers and folk musicians through a "gritty" narrative of American life, Jackson's pursuit was to understand a similar phenomenon through observations of the ordinary American landscape.

Most essentially, Jackson defined landscape as "a concrete, three-dimensional shared reality."[18] He was initially drawn to the idea of landscape through the work of French human geographers, which he encountered when working as an intelligence officer in France during World War II. Through this work, Jackson came to see landscape as a medium through which one could read culture. But this was just the starting point for Jackson, whose writing in *Landscape* would evolve beyond these precedents in geographic thought. In a later essay called "The Word Itself," Jackson insisted that "a landscape is not a natural feature of the environment but a synthetic space, a man-made system of spaces superimposed on the land," and then later in the same passage, "a space deliberately created to speed up or slow down the process of nature."[19] Here it might seem that Jackson is engaging in the work of purification, insisting on a distinction between nature and (synthetic) culture; however, Jackson's focus on the synthetic countered the dominant narrative of the time, which saw landscape as largely made up of non-human nature. "The true solution," as Jackson explained, "[was] a redefinition of nature, eliminating this artificial separation."[20]

While most Americans at mid-century—regardless of their familiarity with the forces shaping their environment—could easily identify the city as modern, few urban dwellers contemplated the countryside in such terms. The dualisms of modernity required equal and opposite forces to play out against each other. According to this reasoning the opposite of the city was the countryside, and the countryside was for many the same as landscape. If the city was a representation of the progressive future, landscape represented a romantic past; if the city was an intensively constructed man-made environment, landscape was a (mostly) natural green oasis. For many Americans at mid-century, landscape could only be understood as a palliative to the realities of the modern environment, a green softening of the hard edges of modernity. The only solution provided by landscape was to be the antithesis of everything that people found disagreeable about their environments. As Jackson critiqued:

> The more the city expands and absorbs us, the firmer the belief in a rural paradise becomes . . . and the result is a popular image of rural America which bears a decreasing resemblance to reality. We see it as a pleasant, drowsy region where old fashioned people are engaged in a kind of work less essential and less profitable with every passing year, but where life has an elemental simplicity and truth. On a more sophisticated (though no better informed) level the countryside is seen as a vast wildlife preserve resounding with birdsong, threaded by sparkling streams—ideal for recreation and something environmental

designers like to label "open space." However we look at it, this hinterland is held to be the great antidote, spiritual as well as physical, to the evils of the city. As long as it survives unchanged we ourselves can hope to survive; urban existence is a kind of purgatory.[21]

One of the themes to which Jackson returned repeatedly was how modern the *entire* American landscape had become—including, most surprisingly, the rural landscape. Jackson recognized that the reality of America's rural locations, rather than representing stability and unchanging values, was one of declining population, technological innovation and radical environmental transformation. Because Jackson saw the entire American landscape as modern, he did not treat the rural landscape as the antithesis of the metropolis. Instead, he saw the logics of modernity (including mechanization, efficiency of movement, and topographic homogenization) in some of the least expected places. Modernity had not confined itself to the obvious locations of urban centers and industrial zones. In fact, Jackson argued in numerous commentaries that some of the most remote and least populated landscapes in the United States were sites of rampant modernization: "It so happens that the American rural landscape is composed not only of forests and lakes and mountains, but of farms and feedlots and irrigation ditches and orchards and tractor agencies and rangeland. It is a place of work, and because it is a place of work, hard and not always rewarding, it is at present undergoing a revolution in its way as radical as the revolution in the urban environment."[22] Jackson saw high-modernist ideology embedded in the landscapes of rural America: in the increasingly uniform plant varieties, the rectangular fields, the new machines for processing, and the new techniques for weed control. He also saw this ideology on the highway strip: in the chain supermarket, the highway motels, and the increasingly abandoned buildings of small town America.[23] But his impulse was always towards the function and impact of these changes in people's daily lives. Jackson was never quick to jump to conclusions about what should or shouldn't be; rather he wanted to understand these landscapes pragmatically, asking questions about their complexity, their draw, and their particular social, economic, and cultural functions.

Importantly, Jackson's work not only insisted on seeing modernity in some of these most "natural" of places, he also drew attention to the modern city as shaped by nature, extending the "proliferation of hybrids" into the urban scene. His writing in *Landscape* demonstrated how "nature is actually omnipresent in the city: in the city's climate, topography, and vegetation . . . [and how] we are in fact surrounded by an impalpable or invisible landscape of spaces and color and light and sound and movement and temperature, in the city no less than the country."[24] Moreover, in his insistence on defining nature as not separate nor separable from human experience, we can see too that this hybrid understanding of nature and culture also came to define the way that he understood the (bodied) self: "What is more, there is a constant action and reaction between ourselves and this environment, so constant indeed that the line between what is environment and what is response to environment is sometimes hard to draw. We are beginning to learn that the world surrounding us affects every aspect of our being, that far from being spectators of the world, we are participants in it."[25] In short, then, the term everyday modernities captures Jackson's contribution to the idea that the modern landscape is a lived, hybrid space, made up of the relationships between active participants, both human and non-human, as they navigate, react to, and reproduce modernity. In the sections that follow I trace the concept of everyday modernities through several of Jackson's key works, focusing on two ideas: the other-directedness of landscapes, and the "bodied" landscape of hot-rodding. The first examines how Jackson's focus on everyday modernities was built through his attention to social relationships, including people's relationship to the land. The second explores how Jackson conceptualized everyday modernities in somatic and kinesthetic terms, focusing on the body's physical relationship to new, twentieth-century technologies of mobility.

THE OTHER-DIRECTEDNESS OF LANDSCAPE

Throughout much of his writing in *Landscape*, Jackson was immersed in a mid-twentieth century milieu of social and cultural criticism that found American mass culture a fascinating focal point for exploring American values, taste, and patterns of consumption. During the 1950s and 1960s, imagery of the material culture of everyday life became pervasive in the media. Post-war affluence and popular culture began to draw attention away from elite tastemakers. Modernity for many had come to mean the conveniences of consumer culture: television, processed foods, timesaving appliances. Madison Avenue worked to spin these new products into the very fabric of American life. As such, cultural modernism was losing its radical edge and was increasingly associated with sterile conformity. Ironically, the sheer pervasiveness of the material conveniences of modernity had transformed modern places (office buildings, suburban homes) and products (cereal, TVs) into the banal reality of everyday life.

In this context, popular books and articles by academics and public intellectuals that documented the rapidly changing American experience found an eager audience—first as confirmation of postwar American exceptionalism,[26] then as an anxious reflection of concern for the fragility or illusion of that exceptionalism. As more Americans found themselves moving up a ladder whose rungs demarcated social class, many became obsessed with acquiring the requisite level of taste, manners and possessions to indicate their position. Russell Lynes' tongue-in-cheek "*Highbrow, Lowbrow, Middlebrow*" and *The Tastemakers*, provided Americans with a parlor game of sorts, placing themselves within such categorizations.[27] Some intellectuals responded to such anxieties over social position with a concern about homogenous mass conformity and consumption.[28] However, not all of these critics were so quick to condemn the emerging consumer habits of the middle class. One of the earliest social observers to document nonjudgmentally how American culture was changing in the postwar period was David Riesman. As evidenced by several of J. B. Jackson's essays from the 50's, Riesman was an important influence on how Jackson began to understand changes in the modern American landscape. Specifically, Riesman's writing helped to demonstrate how modernity could be found in the everyday.

In Jackson's essay "Other-Directed Houses" from the winter 1956–57 issue of *Landscape* he co-opts Riesman's pivotal sociological deconstruction of the American character in *The Lonely Crowd*. Riesman and his co-authors based their observations on "our experiences of living in America—the people we have met, the jobs we have held, the books we have read, the movies we have seen, and the landscape."[29] Central to Riesman's argument was his historical construction of three phases of American character that he termed the tradition-directed, the inner-directed and the other-directed. "Tradition-directed" described a pre-modern, community-based American character before the forces of rapid progress required the cultivation of an "inner-directed," somewhat isolated, American individual working toward advancement in an industrial economy. "Other-directedness" was described by Riesman as the result of "reaching a point at which resources become plentiful enough or are utilized effectively enough to permit a rapid accumulation of capital,"[30] at which point Americans became more concerned with outward expressions of the self and with conforming to the cues broadcast by peer groups and the media. Perhaps assuming that Riesman's work was well known by any educated reader, Jackson extended his concept of the transition from inner-directedness to other-directedness to describe a new American highway landscape struggling for attention:

> I am inclined to believe, however, that we have become entirely too fastidious, too conformist, in architectural matters. In our recently acquired awareness of architectural values we have somehow lost sight of the fact that there is still such a thing as a popular taste in art quite distinct from the educated taste, and that popular taste often evolves in its own way. . . . In all those streamlined facades, in all those flamboyant entrances and deliberately bizarre decorative effects, those cheerfully self-assertive masses of color and light and movement that clash so roughly with the old and traditional there are, I believe, certain underlying characteristics which suggest that we are confronted not by a debased and cheapened art, but by a kind of folk art in mid-XX Century garb. . . . Here every business has to woo the public—a public, moreover, which passes by at forty miles or more an hour—if it is to survive. The result is an *other-directed architecture.*[31]

Jackson utilizes Riesman's idea of other-directedness here to defend the modern highway strip that so many others considered to be gaudy blemishes on the American landscape. His defense insists upon understanding the changing social relationships—that is, the (40mph) other-directedness—out of which these strips have emerged. It is interesting to note that Jackson's reading of Riesman's argument did not adhere to the prevalent critical response to the book that saw it as an unequivocal indictment of modern consumer culture and conformity. In Riesman's Preface to the 1969 edition, he goes to great pains to defend against this over-simplification and instead emphasizes how other-directedness was really about a society that had become inextricably interconnected, in many ways for the better:

> *The Lonely Crowd* advocates the morally and practically difficult enter-prise of living at once on two-levels: that of ideals and even utopian visions and that of day-to-day existence. Our daily life and our ideal-ism must nourish and speak to each other . . . the best hope for change in the direction of our ideals does not lie in efforts at total improve-ment in oneself and in society but in patient work toward incremental changes in the light of a tentative sense of many possible futures.[32]

Here it is easy to see a shared pragmatism between Riesman's view of American society and Jackson's view of the American landscape. Both were interested in the visions of (high-) modernist ideology, but never in isolation from the daily realities in which those visions played out—for better or worse.

"Other-Directed Houses" was not the first time Jackson employed Riesman's tripartite historical narrative of the American character. In 1953's "The Westward-Moving House: Three American Houses and the People Who Lived in Them," Jackson describes (again without directly acknowledging Riesman's book) a similar transformation of the American family's relationship to the land in the 1650s, 1850s and 1950s.[33] Corresponding with Riesman's description of the traditional-directed American character, Jackson describes how the colonists of the 1650s created the "domestic village with its established hierarchy and its working together on common tasks"[34] as a shelter from "an unredeemed wilderness inhabited by savages."[35] By the 1850s, the village-dwellers of earlier generations had moved west and created a dispersed landscape that expressed an independence and ambition for personal and economic (inner-directed) improvement. Jackson il-lustrates the latest stage of family life and its relationship to the land by relating the story of the modern farmer Ray, the descendant of the first two families. "Ray's identity like the identity of the land, has become alarmingly mobile and subject to rapid change."[36] Both identities could be described by Riesman as other-directed, where the family's relationship to the farm is mediated by technology and the increasing connection to national and global markets. As Ray sees it, the farm "is to be an instrument for the prompt and efficient conversion of natural energy in the form of chemical fertilizers or water or tractor fuel or man hours or whatever into energy in the form of cash or further credit—into economic energy, in a word."[37]

Jackson's description here is not an indictment of the modern farmer. Far from it, Jackson frequently insisted on understanding the rural landscape as a place of work, and thus the motivations of farmers as a product of their socio-economic relationships. In a later essay called "The Engineered Environment," Jackson returns to conceptualize the farmer as perpetually "a designer of environments." Similar to his forebears, Jackson explains, ". . . as a product of this century the modern farmer is designing by means of constant experimentation. If present techniques backfire he will not hesitate to drop them in favor of others. Dollars are what he is after, of course; but he is also after something like an insight into the truth."[38]

Jackson was not himself a sociologist, but he drew upon sociological theories like Riesman's "other-directedness" in order to read sociology into the everyday American landscape. He did so because he saw the modern landscape come alive through the social and environmental relationships—and motivations—of mid-century Americans. Where others saw obnoxious eyesores and troubling transformation, Jackson saw sociological and geographic questions about the relationships that produce daily life in mid-century America. Of the highway strip, he asked: "What businesses . . . comprise it? Why is it that certain enterprises proliferate in certain areas and not in others, why are some of them clustered together, and others are far apart? Which of them are dependent on the nearby towns and city, which of them depend on transients?"[39] He also was, at times, attentive to the body's relationship to these places—to how they feel, and to the productiveness of these feelings. Indeed, "tourist traps or not" he insisted, when traveling through empty desert or prairie, roadside establishments are a very welcome sight, and "even the commands to EAT, COME AS YOU ARE, GAS UP, GET FREE ICE WATER AND STICKERS [have] a *comforting* effect."[40] Jackson's attention to the feeling, sensing body is the subject of the following section.

Moving beyond Riesman, Jackson shared with many others—writers, poets, artists, journalists, and intellectuals—a common desire to represent the daily realities of modern American experience, and furthermore, an insistence that those daily realities were an appropriate focus for intellectual theorization and artistic expression. Importantly, Jackson's work in *Landscape* not only legitimized the everyday landscape as a suitably intellectual topic, but also solidified "landscape studies" as a transdisciplinary field.[41] Jackson read widely, in many languages, in both the popular press and the academy, though he purposefully wrote in an accessible style. Because of his (then unique) ability to pull social theory and cultural critique into discussions of landscape, Jackson is widely considered the founder of landscape studies. Here, then, Jackson's influence on contemporary understandings of landscape is quite obvious. Through his writing in *Landscape* magazine, Jackson paved the way for thinking-through landscape as a hybrid concept, where abstract social theories that were not originally conceived in relationship to landscape—including that of "other-directedness"—could become grounded in everyday places, rendering landscape both a concept relevant to many disciplines and a topic appropriate for interdisciplinary study.

THE HOT-RODDER AND THE BODIED LANDSCAPE

The new landscape, seen at a rapid, sometimes even terrifying pace, is composed of rushing air, shifting lights, clouds, waves, a constantly moving, changing horizon. . . . The view is no longer static; it is a revolving, uninterrupted panorama of 360 degrees. In short, the traditional perspective, the traditional way of seeing and experiencing the world is abandoned; in its stead we become active participants, the shifting focus of a moving, abstract world; our nerves and muscles are all of them brought into play. To the perceptive individual, there can be an almost mystical quality to the experience; his identity seems for the moment to be transmuted.[42]

In one of his most iconic essays, "The Abstract World of the Hot-Rodder," J. B. Jackson brought his critical eye to how mobility and speed were transforming the way Americans viewed the landscape.[43] Eschewing either a celebratory or a scorning tone, Jackson painted a picture of how everyday Americans—especially youth—were finding little satisfaction in the quiet contemplation of picturesque and natural scenery and were instead seeking out dynamic new forms of adventure and recreational activities that propelled them through the landscape, often at great speed. The popularization of recreational devices that encouraged "individual means of locomotion" even prior to the wider affordability of automobile and plane travel—skis, sailboats, canoes ("*faltboots*"), bicycles, motorcycles—marked "the dawn of a new era" and a move away from passive forms of nature appreciation. Dating this new era as beginning "about 30 years ago" (approximately the late 1920s), Jackson described ambivalence to the passing of the old relationship to nature: "The layman's former relationship to nature . . . was largely determined by a kind of classic perspective and by awe. A genuine sense of worship precluded any desecration but it also precluded any desire for participation, any intuition that man also belonged. The experience was genuine enough, but it was filtered and humanized; it was rarely immediate."[44]

The desire for an immediate, active engagement with the environment broke with romantic scenic notions of nature appreciation: landscape was now something to be appreciated kinesthetically. After World War II Jackson observed the increasing growth of new sports like "skin-diving, parachute-jumping, surf-riding, outboard motorboating, hot-rod racing, spelunking" as well as water skiing.[45] At the extreme were sports like drag racing on the Bonneville Salt Flats, that simplified the experience of movement to its most essential and stripped down form; a destination no longer required. What connected all of these sports was a desire for speed—a speed that obscured the visual details of the surrounding landscape, elevating feeling above sight. Thus, as Jackson explained, the world of the hot-rodder was "abstract" because visual detail gave way to "a world of flowing movement, blurred light, rushing wind or water."[46]

The participants in this form of abstract travel, Jackson contended, had much in common with the modern artist and architect seeking to simplify their use of materials and streamline their rendering of space; the difference, crucially, was the accessibility of these experiences to everyday people. For Jackson, these new adventurers would

> eventually enrich our understanding of ourselves with a new poetry and a new nature mysticism. I would not go so far as to say that the Wordsworth of the second half of the 20th Century must be a graduate of the drag-strip, or that a motorcycle is a necessary adjunct to any modern "Excursion"; but I earnestly believe that whoever he is and whenever he appears he will have to express some of the uncommunicated but intensely felt joys of that part of American culture if he is to interpret completely our relationship to the world around us.[47]

Here it is clear that, for Jackson, the desire for speed suggested a new poetics of movement for the common man, one where the visceral experience of movement itself was paramount.[48] Through this new lens, Jackson demonstrated how modernity became literally embodied via the (increasingly) everyday experience of speed. The hot-rodder himself was just one example among several as Jackson sought to consider the different ways that one can experience (and indeed *produce*) the landscape through rapid bodily movement. Importantly, however, the "natural" environment itself was not absent from this world of abstract travel. Rather, these modern technologies ironically provided young Americans with a renewed and invigorated relationship to "nature." Jackson explained that because these rapid sports entail some kind of (not wholly unpleasant) sense of danger, they also produce a heightened alertness to surrounding conditions, many of which are felt: "air currents, shifts of wind and temperature, the texture of snow, the firmness of the track."[49] In his discussion, the hot-rodder (typology) therefore becomes a sort of hybrid figure, in which the sensory abilities of the everyday body merge with the abstraction of modern speed, producing a landscape that is inseparable from the active people that move through it. As the opening quotation of this section observes, in this version of landscape "our nerves and muscles are all of them brought into play."

Although "The Abstract World of the Hot-Rodder" was Jackson's only essay that dedicated such direct attention to the sensing, feeling body, such a body is not absent in his other writing, nor his editorial work in *Landscape*. For example, the beginning of "The Stranger's Path" is full of descriptions that detail what it feels like for a stranger to enter a new city. Jackson explains that these descriptions come from his own, "painfully acquired knowledge of how to appraise strange cities" and from his inability to "derive the slightest spark of inspiration" from the middle class residential quarters of these cities.[50] The path that Jackson describes is, again, a more gritty, everyday place: "loud, taudry, down-at-the-heel, full of dives and small catch-penny businesses."[51] And, it is also a place of exchange: "of goods for cash . . . of talk and drink . . . of mandolins and foreign pistols and diamond rings against cash."[52] Thus, here again we can see Jackson's interest in examining the logics of modernity via the experiences of the everyday—the impulses, desires, sensations, and relationships that make up a stranger's path through the city.

Jackson also welcomed and encouraged writing on bodily sensation and perception in his editorial work for *Landscape*. Specifically, the humanistic geographer Yi-Fu Tuan originally tested his phenomenological ideas in a piece he wrote for *Landscape* called "Topophila or, Sudden Encounter with the Landscape," over a decade before his book on the subject was published.[53] Tuan defined "topophilia" as "the affective bond between people and place or setting."[54] Later in the book, Tuan explains that while landscape (in the 1970s) had seemingly become synonymous with scenery (and thus abstracted from the 'real world'), "a now obsolete meaning of scenery is 'a moving exhibition of feeling.'"[55] It is worth noting that Tuan's work, alongside that of other humanistic geographers, is considered an important precedent to the contemporary "affective turn" in geography and beyond. And indeed, we can also see traces of Jackson's thinking in this turn, where the sensing, feeling body quite literally *matters* in the production of space. The popularity of "non-representational theory"[56] and "actor network theory,"[57] for example, exhibits an attention to the hybrid, relational way in which bodies—both human and non-human—produce the world as an ever-changing series of material inter-relationships. In this network of "things," the human body has co-evolved with other things, producing a world of hybrid distributions.[58] Drawing on architectural theorist Sanford Kwinter, affect geographer Nigel Thrift notes that this emphasis on things questions the solidity of the world, since so much of it is ultimately mutable, working according to a spectrum of different time scales (Grosz 2005). Increasingly, many human activities seem to realize this. Indeed, it is a point that has been brilliantly made by Kwinter (2001). Thus Kwinter points to the rise of a whole series of sports that depend on an artful shaping of the different time scales of the environment for sustenance, tracking and tracing flows and perturbations in order to produce e/affects. *Kwinter mentions paragliding, surfing, snowboarding and rock-climbing as sports of falling that extend a streaming ethos to landscapes, understood as "motorfields of solids."*[59]

Mirroring Jackson's interest in movement and sport, here Thrift details a version of landscape that is very much in line with Jackson's landscape of active participants. Indeed, Jackson's attention to not only (human) bodies but also things like air currents and shifts of wind reveals an interest in the production of hybrid realities that dovetails with Thrift's insistence that the human body is not separate from the world of things. And there is even a sense of "everydayness" in Thrift's writing when he insists that embodiment is not just about honed skills and the purposeful cultivation (of experience) but is also "[about] tripping, falling over, and a whole host of other such mistakes."[60] While few if any affect theorists credit the work of Jackson (or Tuan) in the genealogies of their thought, it is clear that parallels exist between these contemporary writings and those in Jackson's *Landscape* over half a century earlier. The point, however, is not to criticize or ponder the lack of cited antecedents, but instead to demonstrate the connections that can be made by tracing the everyday modernities that are made visible through Jackson's work.

CONCLUSIONS: LOOKING BACK/LOOKING FORWARD

Landscape makes us conscious of relatives even in the awkwardness of new beginnings in our way of life. It does not demand beauty but new natural laws from which beauty may emerge. *Landscape*, through its thoughtful selection of subjects, stimulates dedication in the professions concerned about environment.[61]

Jackson's unique voice and stimulating ideas resonated with many—from professionals and scholars to the "intelligent layman."[62] In the tenth anniversary issue of *Landscape*, the great twentieth-century architect Louis Kahn wrote the above short (and somewhat cryptic) note suggesting an appreciation for Jackson's ability to find beauty and meaning in unexpected places—places many others might describe as ugly or backward or dilapidated or prosaic or irrelevant, but that both Jackson and Kahn found inspiring and worthy of further understanding. The note also spoke to Jackson's focus on connections—from the relationships between people and land to the trans-disciplinary thinking that fueled both his writing and editorial work—and to his insistence on understanding the newness of the present in pragmatic, lived terms.

From architecture, landscape architecture, planning, and geography, to history, philosophy, sociology, anthropology, and more, the scope and reach of J. B. Jackson's work in *Landscape* is truly remarkable. Through his writing and editorial work, Jackson forged paths and established connections that would reflect the tenor of academic scholarship on landscape for years to come. While not all of those who came after read, or cited, his work when crafting their own scholarship, it is clear that Jackson often anticipated momentous shifts in theorization, sometimes decades earlier.

In this paper, I have argued that J. B. Jackson's work on the modern American landscape has both historical and contemporary relevance. More specifically, through the concept of "everyday modernities," I have defined and specified how Jackson sought to reconcile the logics of modernity with the everyday, lived realities of mid-century American life. This concept also has helped to demonstrate the continued significance of Jackson's work to contemporary theorizing: on everyday landscape, the material or affective body, hybrid geographies, and more. Indeed, through Jackson's work not only can we locate the precedents of much contemporary theorizing on these subjects, we can also see the history of the mid-century modern American landscape with renewed importance.

Of course, this is not to say that Jackson's work is to be free from critique. To be sure, there are many differences between the work of mid-century scholars and those of today, and Jackson's writing and editorial work for *Landscape* is a product of its time: when diverse voices were rare and the male pronoun represented all of humankind. Nevertheless, through the concept of everyday modernities, it is possible to argue for Jackson's continued relevance as a way of (re-)reading both the present and the past. As Latour said of his own project:

> As soon as we direct our attention simultaneously to the work of purification and the work of hybridization, we immediately stop being wholly modern, and our future begins to change. At the same time we stop having been modern, because we become retrospectively aware that the two sets of practices have always already been at work in the historical period that is ending. Our past begins to change. Finally, if we have never been modern—at least in the way criticism tells the story—the tortuous relations that we have maintained with the other nature-cultures would also be transformed.[63]

To be sure, Jackson's goal was not to prove that we have never been modern; rather his work suggests that all landscapes—utopian and everyday, urban and rural, in the past and today—have been products of, and productive of, modernity. At the same time, like Latour, Jackson was interested in attending to the work of both purification and hybridization. He sketched an approach to the modern landscape that took seriously these binaries of modernist ideology, but sought to highlight the complex networks and connections—the hybrid spaces—that produce the material realities of everyday life. Jackson fashioned a way of understanding the modern landscape that—like Latour's provocative statement above—enabled new ways of considering the past, present, and future. Indeed, the first book Jackson wrote soon after stepping down from the editorship of *Landscape, American Space: The Centennial Years*, demonstrated the potential to re-read past landscapes. In the book, Jackson described how an emerging American landscape after the Civil War was increasingly characterized by a new conception of space. It is in this period that Jackson found the origin of particular forms of twentieth-century American modernity, where the concept of space as something to be enclosed and delimited by boundaries was challenged by new open forms that allowed for the organized and systemic flow and movement of raw materials, natural resources and people. The modern sensibilities of the engineer, the scientist and the industrialist combined to transform the land and the way Americans saw their landscape.[64]

Extending the modern landscape idea into the present, the concept of everyday modernities captures an approach that can help students, practitioners, and theorists to read the modern landscape anew. Of course, what we mean by modernity today has been radically transformed by post-industrial economies, ever-evolving technologies, and the virtual landscapes of cyberspace; however, all of these emergent realities are creating new patterns in the landscape, in obvious and not so obvious ways. While Jackson's particular lens was certainly a very personal one, extending from his own life experiences and points of view (with all the advantages and limitations that that embodies), his opened-minded search for these patterns can help to reveal new connections and inspire new questions about the evolving modern American landscape.

JEFFREY BLANKENSHIP is an assistant professor of architectural studies at Hobart and William Smith Colleges in Geneva, NY where he teaches the history of modern landscape architecture and design studios. His recently published works have appeared in *Landscape Journal*, and *ACME*.

NOTES

1. See D. W. Meinig, "Reading the Landscape: An Appreciation of W. G. Hoskins and J. B. Jackson," in *The Interpretation of Ordinary Landscapes: Geographical Essays*, ed. D. W. Meinig (New York: Oxford University Press, 1979): 210–237; Peirce Lewis, "Learning from Looking: Geographic and Other Writing About the American Cultural Landscape," *American Quarterly* 35, No. 3 (1983): 242–261; Helen Lefkowitz Horowitz, "J. B. Jackson and the Discovery of the American Landscape," in *Landscape in Sight: Looking at American*, ed. Helen Lefkowitz Horowitz (New Haven: Yale University Press, 1997): ix–xxxi; Paul Groth, "Frameworks for Cultural Landscape Study," in *Understanding Ordinary Landscapes*, Paul Groth and Todd W. Bressi, eds. (New Haven: Yale University Press, 1997): 1–21; Paul Groth and Chris Wilson, "The Polyphony of Cultural Landscape Study," in *Everyday America: Cultural Landscape Studies After J. B. Jackson*, Chris Wilson and Paul Groth, eds. (Berkeley: University of California Press, 2003): 1–22; and Chris Wilson, "A Life on the Stranger's Path," in *Drawn to Landscape: The Pioneering Work of J. B. Jackson*,

Janet Mendelsohn and Chris Wilson, eds. (Virginia: George F. Thompson Publishing, 2015): 19–31.

2. Chris Wilson, "A Life on the Stranger's Path," 19–21.

3. Helen Lefkowitz Horowitz, "J. B. Jackson and the Discovery of the American Landscape," xvi.

4. In the biographical essays noted above, Paul Groth, Helen Horowitz, and Chris Wilson have all documented the numerous pseudonyms that Jackson used, noting that Jackson exclusively authored the first two issues (Horowitz, xxiv); possibly the first two years (Wilson, 27). These pseudonyms provided the cover for Jackson to try out different literary voices.

5. See note 1.

6. *Everyday America: Cultural Landscape Studies After J. B. Jackson*, Chris Wilson and Paul Groth, eds. (Berkeley: University of California Press, 2003); *Drawn to Landscape: The Pioneering Work of J. B. Jackson*, Janet Mendelsohn and Chris Wilson, eds. (Virginia: George F. Thompson Publishing, 2015).

7. Patricia Nelson Limerick, "J. B. Jackson and the Play of the Mind: Inquiry and Assertion as Contact Sports," in *Everyday America: Cultural Landscape Studies After J. B. Jackson*, Chris Wilson and Paul Groth, eds. (Berkeley: University of California Press, 2003): 27–36.

8. Meinig, "Reading the Landscape," 235.

9. Denis, Cosgrove, *Social Formation and Symbolic Landscape* (Madison: University of Wisconsin Press, 1998 [1984]): 1. In this work Cosgrove makes a strong argument for landscape as a "way of seeing that has its own history" (1).

10. James C. Scott, *Seeing Like a State: How Certain Schemes to Improve the Human Condition Have Failed* (New Haven: Yale University Press, 1998): 4.

11. Ibid., 6.

12. Neil Brenner and Nik Theodore, "Cities and the Geographies of 'Actually Existing Neoliberalism,'" *Antipode* 34, No. 3 (July 2002): 349–379.

13. Bruno Latour, *We Have Never Been Modern* (Cambridge: Harvard University Press, 1993).

14. Ibid., 10–11.

15. Ibid., 7.

16. For example, Jane Jacob's argument in favor of the everyday vibrancy of Greenwich Village over the lifeless environments created by urban renewal policy in *The Death and Life of Great American Cities* (New York: Random House, 1961).

17. cf., Henri Lefebvre, *The Critique of Everyday Life*, Volume 1, John Moore, trans. (London: Verso, 1991 (1947). Although Lefebvre is talking about the production of capitalism, Jackson avoided overt references to capitalism and its role in the production and reproduction of modern landscapes such as the highway strip.

18. J. B. Jackson, "The Word Itself," in *Discovering the Vernacular Landscape* (New Haven: Yale University Press, 1984): 5.

19. Ibid., 8.

20. J. B. Jackson, "Notes and Comments," *Landscape: Magazine of Human Geography* 10, no. 1 (Fall 1960), 2.

21. J. B. Jackson, "An Engineered Environment," *Landscape* 16, no. 1 (Autumn 1966), 16.

22. Ibid.

23. Ibid., 19.

24. J. B. Jackson, "Notes and Comments," *Landscape: Magazine of Human Geography* 10, no. 1 (Fall 1960), 2.

25. Ibid.

26. cf. Henry Steele Commager, *The American Mind: An Interpretation of American Thought and Character Since the 1880s* (New Haven: Yale University Press, 1950).

27. Russell Lynes, "Highbrow, Lowbrow, Middlebrow," *Harpers* (February 1949), 19–28; *The Tastemakers* (New York: Harper, 1954).

28. For example, see William H. White, *The Organization Man* (New York: Simon and Schuster, 1956); Sloan Wilson, *The Man in the Gray Flannel Suit* (New York: Simon and Schuster, 1955).

29. David Riesman, with Nathan Glazer and Reuel Denney, *The Lonely Crowd: A Study of the Changing American Character* (New Haven: Yale University Press, 1950), xxi.

30. Ibid., 19.

31. J. B. Jackson, "Other-Directed Houses," *Landscape: Magazine of Human Geography* 6, no. 2 (Winter 1956–1957), 31.

32. Riesman, *The Lonely Crowd*, (1969), xx.

33. J. B. Jackson, "The Westward-Moving House," *Landscape: Magazine of Human Geography* 2, no. 3 (Spring 1953), 8–21.

34. Ibid., 9.

35. Ibid., 11.

36. Ibid., 21.

37. Ibid., 20.

38. Jackson, "An Engineered Environment," 20.

39. Jackson, "Other-Directed Houses," 30.

40. Ibid., 29.

41. Groth, "Frameworks for Cultural Landscape Study," 18.

42. J. B. Jackson, "The Abstract World of the Hot-Rodder," *Landscape: Magazine of Human Geography* 7, no. 2 (Winter 1957–1958), 25.

43. Ibid., 22–27.

44. Ibid., 24.

45. Ibid.

46. Ibid., 26.

47. Ibid., 27.

48. Literary scholar Enda Duffy, in *The Speed Handbook: Velocity, Pleasure, Modernism* (Durham: Duke University Press, 2009), builds on Aldous Huxley's claim that the only new pleasure invented by modernity was speed. Duffy argues for the existence of an "adrenaline aesthetic" (3) in which he theorizes that speed—especially via the automobile—represented an opportunity for the masses to "feel" modernity in their bones.

49. Jackson, "Abstract World," 25.

50. J. B. Jackson, "The Stranger's Path." *Landscape: Magazine of Human Geography* 7 (Autumn 1957): 11.

51. Ibid., 12.

52. Ibid.

53. Yi-Fu Tuan, "Topophilia or, sudden encounter with the landscape," *Landscape* 11, no. 1 (Fall 1961), 29–32.
54. Yi-Fu Tuan, *Topophilia: A Study of Environmental Perception, Attitudes, and Values* (New York: Columbia University Press, 1974), 4.
55. Ibid., 133.
56. Nigel Thrift, *Non-Representational Theory: Space, Politics, Affect* (London: Routledge, 2007).
57. Sarah Whatmore, *Hybrid Geographies: Natures, Cultures, Spaces* (London: Sage Publications, 2002).
58. Thrift, *Non-Representational Theory*, 11.
59. Ibid., emphasis added.
60. Ibid., 10.
61. Louis Kahn, "10th Anniversary Letters," *Landscape: Magazine of Human Geography* 10, no. 1. (Fall 1960), 4.
62. Jackson, J. B. *Landscape: Human Geography of the Southwest* 1 (Spring 1951): inside cover.
63. Latour, *We Have Never Been Modern*, 10–11.
64. J. B. Jackson, *American Space: The Centennial Years, 1865–1876* (New York: Norton, 1972).

Towards a Pluralistic Understanding of the Mediating Concept of Wilderness

JASON P. MATZKE

Abstract

This paper addresses the current debate in environmental ethics regarding the notion of wilderness. It has been argued by J. Baird Callicott and Michael Nelson, William Cronon, and others that our current idea of wilderness is deeply flawed, especially insofar as it draws a sharp dichotomy between us and the rest of nature. This paper first explores what it means (and what it does not) to say that "wilderness" is a constructed concept. It then describes some of the key objections and solutions proposed in order to argue that the best approach to understanding the concept and place of wilderness is to embrace a pluralistic approach. This proposal would allow for mutually inconsistent and incommensurable ideas to co-exist without succumbing to the pitfalls of an anything-goes relativism.

INTRODUCTION

Our experience of the world is mediated in a variety of ways. In the most simple sense, our minds fill in the gaps, so to speak, to provide us with images of the world that exceed, or restructure, the raw data we receive through the senses. As René Descartes notes in his *Meditations on First Philosophy*, we "see" a person dressed in clothes and a hat walking away from us despite that upon more careful inspection the sensations we have are only of the clothes, hat, and movement of these, with no person literally visible.[1] Similarly, John Locke supposed that somehow (though he was not sure exactly how) our minds perceive from an object's primary qualities (e.g., surface texture) properties such as color, which are not in the object in any literal sense.[2] David Hume with causation, Immanuel Kant with space and time, and others too numerous to mention—both before and after—have wrestled with the philosophical question of how it is that the world appears to us as it does despite it not actually being as we perceive it. The mind interprets, shapes, and constructs our experience; our categories, ideas, concepts, and emotions mediate the world for us. Although we have rejected Descartes' transcendent, "neutral" observer, his observation regarding what we "see" when we perceive the moving clothes and hat is consistent with our contemporary view of ourselves as fully embodied, immersed, and part of the world we seek to know. Inherent in this, though, is also the realization that the concepts—the categories through which we experience and organize our experiences—are often deeply flawed. Sometimes they are internally inconsistent; sometimes they fail to conform with our other beliefs or values; and sometimes they have harmful practical implications.

In the past twenty-or-so years, worries about the mediating concept of "wilderness" have emerged as an important subplot in the wider interdisciplinary field of environmental ethics. Some have argued that—at least as it has arisen in the European-North American context—the idea of wilderness is so flawed that it needs to be radically reworked or even abandoned for an alternative. In a provocative and widely read essay, Ramachandra Guha argued in 1989 that when the Americanized notion of wilderness, positing as it does a sharp dichotomy between humans and the rest of nature, is exported as a conservation model to other regions, it leads to the displacement of those who are most immediately dependent upon their local environment—most significantly, the poor.[3] Acknowledging the role Guha's paper played in spurring on the current debate, J. Baird Callicott and Michael Nelson argue that part of the problem lies in our thinking "that the word *wilderness*, like the word *mountain*, [is] the innocuous and unproblematic English name for something that exists in the world independently of any socially constructed skein of ideas." Instead, the "received wilderness idea," as they so aptly call it—our inherited notion of wilderness—mediates our experience of the world, sometimes in quite negative and even incoherent ways.[4] In typical academic fashion, the push and pull of arguments about the meaning and usefulness of wilderness have played out (and were already playing out) slowly since Guha's paper. It is time to both acknowledge the progress made and to suggest a next step, which to my mind is to look for a way to make coherent the seemingly valuable but inconsistent responses to the wilderness problem.

Two decades of debate have unfolded around three key questions: What does it mean to say that wilderness is a concept? What is wrong with the concept as it is usually held? And, can the concept be salvaged—cleansed of its problematic elements—or is it in need of replacement?[5] In what follows, I take these questions more-or-less in turn to suggest that the mediating concept of wilderness should be thought of in pluralistic terms. That is, there need not be a single, monistic concept (or replacement concept) in order to have a theoretically and practically well-functioning concept; the idea of wilderness might coherently include a variety of even mutually inconsistent or incommensurable notions. A key part of the argument here will rely on William Cronon's proposal to allow for flexibility in how we think about the humanized elements of wilderness. This is best seen in his notion of a "historical wilderness," a concept he develops as a solution to the erasures of signs of human intervention that he fears will occur as the Apostle Islands National Lakeshore transitioned in 2004 to a legally designated wilderness area. This case illustrates nicely how a particularly problematic element of the received wilderness idea—the sharp dichotomy it presupposes and perpetuates between us and the rest of nature—might be addressed. Differently motivated but concerned as well with the problems of the received wilderness idea, Callicott and Nelson's (especially Callicott's own) proposed solutions focus our attention more on ecological necessity than on the benefits of adequately seeing the human history that is comingled with areas we wish to call wilderness. Together the different solutions motivate the call for a pluralistic interpretation of wilderness.

THE DECONSTRUCTION OF "WILDERNESS" PART I

In the opening paragraphs of "The Trouble with Wilderness," William Cronon provides a clear social-constructivist view of wilderness:

> Far from being the one place on earth that stands apart from humanity, [wilderness] is quite profoundly a human creation—indeed, the creation of very particular human cultures at very particular moments

in human history. . . . As we gaze into the mirror it holds up for us, we too easily imagine that what we behold is Nature when in fact we see the reflection of our own unexamined longings and desires.[6]

This view, which need not be so thoroughly socially-constructivist that it rejects the world as a thing in itself, represents an important critical response to the tendency to see wild, unhumanized nature as an objectively existing place of goodness in contrast or as a solution to the degraded human realm. As Cronon puts it, far from being an antidote to our troubled human lives and mal-relationship with nature, "wilderness is itself no small part of the problem."[7] As a vocal advocate of protecting areas of significant natural and ecological value, Cronon clearly does not mean that those areas harm us, but that our conceptualization of such places sets us up for various failures. Most important for Cronon is that the sharp dichotomy between us and the rest of nature inherent in our notion of wilderness can give us "little hope of discovering what an ethical, sustainable, *honorable* human place in nature might actually look like."[8] The fact that wilderness is a mediating concept, and not a straightforward report of the world, is what makes such a problem possible.

It might be objected immediately that wilderness *is* straightforwardly real—or at least that it is no more humanly-constructed than are Locke's colors, depending as the latter do on the way the world and our minds, as opposed to social norms and framings, work. Even if "blue" is just one language-group's word for a range of colors, and even if there is some variation in what each language-group puts into each category of color, the degree of social construction could be minimal. Similarly, one might continue, as macro-beings we experience many of the things in the world of macro-objects as solid and impenetrable despite our belief in a quite different sub-atomic reality: objects *really are* solid when considered as macro-objects in relation to other macro-objects such as ourselves. Wilderness, it will be said, is more like "table," "dog," or "blue" than it is like, say, race or gender—two concepts widely criticized as mere social inventions. Culturally and individually we will have slightly different meanings, expectations, and feelings about dogs—e.g., as best friends and companions, protection or work animals, or even as sources of food—but any conceptual deconstruction of "dog" will not lead to our questioning the animals' existence independent of our concepts. The same is true of wilderness: one can point to it, and despite one's love and another's fear of it, we all know of what we speak and cannot help but see it; it is real and does not change merely because our ideas of it change. Further, many of the current disagreements—for instance, how much wilderness remains, which areas might be good candidates for the increased protection that wilderness designation confers, and the extent to which it should be managed—can be contested without fundamental disagreement as to what wilderness is.

Another way of putting this—a view with which I disagree—is that the places we call "wilderness" are the quintessential examples of *non*-mediated space. Wilderness is pure other—completely unhumanized—and as such it is experienced *as itself*. It is not Cronon's mirror in which we see ourselves, but it is distinctly other than human. Unlike even table, which exists in reference to human need (and is usually literally built by us), wilderness is the opposite of all that is human. What is meant here is that although the word "wilderness" functions as a category or class term that particular societies have developed at particular times, our conceptualization of this class—that is, the idea of wilderness—does not construct (or mediate) the *place* for us. It is irrelevant that we did not notice wilderness prior to the expansion of the urban and suburban; it was clearly there as unhumanized place all the while.

This push against Cronon's, and Callicott and Nelson's, social constructivist claims is not necessarily a rejection of the view that concepts are socially constructed, but it is a push to distinguish more sharply between an object and our conceptualizations of that object. One could hold—following Ian Hacking—that different concepts can be related differently to the world, with some being more "merely" constructions (and incidentally, constructions in different ways—consider "credit union" in contrast to "white-tailed deer") and others pointing more obviously to things that exist independently of our thinking about them.[9] Unless they are denying the possibility of social construction altogether—which is *prima facie* untenable—the objectors imagined here would be accepting some constructivist developments but insisting nonetheless that wilderness, at least, is objectively real.

If we spread out the various views on a spectrum, on one end might be the view just described: although we have a concept that describes the place, this concept does very little, if any, mediating. We can call this the "straightforwardly realist" position. Against this view, Cronon spends quite some time describing the extent to which the wilderness concept has changed from one era to another—e.g., from a place of desolation to be feared to sacred space in which one might meet God.[10] Callicott and Nelson outline the same conceptual shift with the same argumentative intent, drawing from Roderick Nash's much earlier book-length treatment of the evolution of the wilderness concept, *Wilderness and the American Mind* (1967).[11] While changes of view do not necessarily mean that a concept is thoroughly constructed in the sense of being minimally limited or shaped by the world (we do, after all, think we can be more or less correct about various claims about the world), the historical malleability of wilderness certainly suggests that it is not just a description of an objectively existing place. "Wilderness" fundamentally contains all sorts of non-empirically testable elements—for example, notions of peace, freedom, divinity, adventure, beauty, and goodness (or the opposites of these).

At the other end of the spectrum would be the view that wilderness is wholly a socially constructed entity; this might be called the "fully constructivist" position. On this view, the concept of wilderness is not at all grounded in the world and hence is, presumably, as malleable as a culture's ideas regarding love, politics, religion, and aesthetics. Cronon notes that some might interpret talk of social construction to mean that "everything become[s] relative to our own ideas and there is no stable ground on which we can hope to make a stand in defending the natural world."[12] Activist and author Dave Foreman worries that wilderness areas will be discredited by those who want to push back on environmental protection.[13] I take him to mean that if wilderness is just in the mind, but development brings tangible goods and money—and if so-called environmental activists and philosophers cannot even agree on its ontological status—the score can be quickly settled in favor of development.

Unsurprisingly, none of the environmental thinkers who challenge the received wilderness idea by in part pointing out its socially-constructed character think that the fully-constructivist position is credible. Cronon, for example, says that although our idea of Yosemite as "a sacred landscape and national symbol is very much a human invention," it is also "a real place in nature." To insist that it exists as either fully objective or mere idea is a false dilemma.[14] Elsewhere he says, "let me hasten to add that the nonhuman world we encounter in wilderness is far from being merely our own invention."[15] Although Callicott clearly takes a constructivist perspective as he argues for re-crafting "wilderness" as "biodiversity reserves," he too pushes back on the fully-constructivist position: "The *idea* of wilderness that we have inherited from Thoreau, Muir, and their successors may be ill conceived, but there's nothing whatever wrong with the *places* that we call wilderness, except that they are too small, too few and far between."[16]

Unless, then, one is a complete skeptic regarding our access to and beliefs about the world, wilderness can be both "real" in the sense that it is not entirely a social construct (there is something there independently of our conceptualizations of it) *and* be socially constructed. That is, to say that something is a social construct does not entail that it is not also "real" in the sense that it picks out something—a dog, for instance—that exists independently of human cognition. It is true that some concepts, such as "race," fail miserably as a biological or moral category, but even it, unfortunately, is as least *experientially* real (although it need not be). But this is not the sense of existence that we are wondering about with respect to wilderness; the debate here is about the extent to which wilderness is real independently of our concepts of it, and the admittedly ambiguous consensus amongst environmental thinkers is that there certainly exist large areas of less-humanized place, easily distinguished from more humanized place, on this planet despite the inherent malleability of our ideas about those places.

THE DECONSTRUCTION OF "WILDERNESS" PART II

If even the most vocal of the academicians critical of wilderness agree to the middle position just described—the "critical realist" position—why are the complaints against the received wilderness idea so often framed in the language of social construction? All concepts are, after all, socially constructed in some way or other. The answer lies in Hacking's observation that no one bothers to make social-constructivist claims unless they are trying to move us to question, alter, or even reject a particular concept.[17] And, of course, this is the case in the current wilderness debate in environmental ethics.

What, then, are the objections to the received wilderness idea? Efforts at deconstruction include objections of three sorts: the concept in question a) is internally inconsistent, b) fails to fit with other (descriptive or normative) beliefs about the world, and c) contains harmful practical implications. To illustrate, let us return to race. It involves the inconsistent beliefs that one must belong to a single racial classification, that this entails quite particular physical, dispositional, mental, and emotional characteristics shared by all members of that group, and that although even a little inheritance from some groups makes a person belong fully to that group, a lot of inheritance from another, privileged group does not. In addition to the incoherence of this set of ideas, race (and the racism often accompanying it) fails also to comport with our other beliefs regarding personal worth, justice, and biology. Finally, it fails in terms of its obvious immoral consequences. Perhaps the consequences are not connected logically, or inherently, to the concept, but in the case of race the historic development and current intertwining of race and racism make the consequences quite firmly contingently connected. The point is not that every objection to a concept must fit neatly into one of these categories. The moral objections, for example, can often be framed either in terms of inconsistency with our moral beliefs or in terms of unacceptable consequences. In fact, objection type (a) and (c) could both be reduced, though with loss of nuance, to (b) since each of these problems is a species of inconsistency between beliefs and commitments, whether descriptive or normative.

Callicott and Nelson, claiming that "the received wilderness idea has been mortally wounded," list several of the objections raised by various authors: "The wilderness idea is alleged to be ethnocentric, androcentric, phallocentric, unscientific, unphilosophic, impolitic, outmoded, even genocidal."[18] The core of Callicott's own objection is that wilderness, especially as it is defined in the 1964 *Wilderness Act*—a place "in contrast with those areas where man and his works dominate" and as "untrammeled by man, where man himself is a visitor who does not remain"—is incoherent.[19] It furthers, he argues, the pre-Darwinian dichotomy between us and the rest of nature, despite us knowing full well that we are part of nature.[20] Cronon also sees the wilderness idea as internally inconsistent in its simultaneously positing a sharp dichotomy between humans and nature while also claiming nonetheless that wilderness is our true home.[21] He notes that "the removal of Indians to create an 'uninhabited wilderness'—uninhabited as never before in the human history of the place—reminds us just how invented, just how constructed, the American wilderness really is."[22] The internal inconsistency is clear: everything about us is both, but yet cannot be, natural and unnatural.

Donald Waller, arguing against Callicott and Nelson's contention that the received wilderness idea is beyond salvage, claims that "some such separation is essential to sustain the many species that cannot tolerate the more denatured habitats that now dominate our landscapes."[23] Similarly, Reed Noss worries that "we not discount the tremendous value of huge, roadless, essentially unmanaged areas: what has been called 'Big Wilderness,'" by pushing too hard against the human/nature dualism.[24] Interestingly, though, objectors to the received wilderness idea, such as Cronon, and Callicott and Nelson, are not suggesting that the solution is to dissolve any and all distinction between us and nature. Callicott takes the strongest stance against the traditional divide between humans and all else, arguing, as indicated above, that such a view has been overthrown by Darwin; yet, even he notes that there is one quite relevant difference: humans have the ability to make choices. Although many of our actions have, as of late, caused much suffering and ecological disruption by virtue of the degree and rapidity (not kind) of changes brought, there is no in-principle reason why we could not make better choices.[25] It is, as Val Plumwood points out, the dualistic, hierarchical, or oppositional understanding, after all, not the marking of a distinction itself that makes the wilderness notion problematic.[26]

Second, wilderness also conflicts, it is said, with our other beliefs about the world. We know, for example, that North America was not an unhumanized "wilderness" when Columbus and other Europeans "discovered" it. William Denevan argues that there were about 54 million people in the Western hemisphere in 1492, enough, he notes, "to dispel any notion of 'empty lands.'" Further, the impact of these people on the environment was significant.[27] The extent to which Puritan settlers saw, relative to Europe, a landscape little affected by the small numbers of indigenous people they encountered was due directly to, Denevan continues, "Old World" diseases, which caused "probably the greatest demographic disaster ever." He reports that between 1492 and 1650, the population of the Americas may have declined by nearly 90 percent.[28] Any depopulation was, then, itself "artificial"—the result of pandemics made possible by European technology and economic and religious ambition. As Callicott points out, the received wilderness idea, by drawing a sharp distinction between humans and the rest of nature, ends up being "woefully ethnocentric" as it must ignore the extent to which indigenous people changed the world around them.[29] This issue becomes especially clear in Cronon's Apostle Islands case described below.

Third, the way we think about wilderness leads to unwanted consequences. For Cronon the principle worry is that "idealizing a distant wilderness too often means not idealizing the environment in which we actually live, the landscape that for better or worse we call home."[30] A different concern regarding the practical consequences of the received wilderness idea can be found in Guha's scathing attack, mentioned above, on the export of the "uniquely American" notion of wilderness (he couches it in terms of Deep Ecology).[31] When wilderness as unhumanized place becomes the operative concept in environmental protection in long-occupied places such as India, it furthers a shift in wealth from the disenfranchised to the wealthy and powerful, including rich tourists. It does so by requiring the depopulation of, or by limiting access to, a place to make it fit the wilderness notion; it favors wilderness, over the needs of local people who have long depended upon an area for firewood, food, and shelter.[32] Similarly, Fabienne Bayet argues that the received wilderness idea potentially harms Australian Aboriginals. Insofar as it "denotes land which is wild, uninhabited, or inhabited only by wild animals," and leads to policies of depopulation of native peoples, it represents "yet another form of paternalism and dispossession," and "dehumanizes the indigenous people living within that landscape."[33]

All three types of problems arise from the fact that the idea of wilderness is so malleable. Through all of the objections, though, one issue keeps coming to the fore: the positing, incoherently, of a sharp divide between us and the rest of nature. Although it is important to maintain some distinction, as we saw above, this should not involve seeing ourselves as different in kind from all other life, free from the constraints and pressures of inhabiting the ecosystems we do. Callicott and Nelson argue that the problems, and I have described only a few from their much longer list cited above, are so serious that it is best to stop conceptualizing the places we want to set aside from human development as "wilderness." We can either, on their view, change the concept radically enough by deanthropocentrizing it that we should rename it—perhaps as "biodiversity reserves" to emphasize the ecological over the human priorities—or we could replace the concept entirely. The latter option would involve substituting for wilderness "the obviously related, but very different, concept of wildness and the concepts of free nature, sustainability, and reinhabitation that are allied with it."[34] I find both of these suggestions attractive in their own way, but before saying more I want to consider Cronon's "historical wilderness" idea.

THE APOSTLE ISLANDS WILDERNESS

In 2004, some 80 percent of the land of Wisconsin's Apostle Islands National Lakeshore was granted federal wilderness status. Twenty-one islands (all of the archipelago but Madeline Island, which contains a small town, an airstrip, a marina, and state and township parks) had been since 1970 part of the National Parks system, thereby already under some degree of environmental protection. Just prior to the granting of wilderness status, Cronon entered the public debate via an essay in *Orion Magazine* entitled, "The Riddle of the Apostle Islands: How do you manage a wilderness full of human stories?" He writes that he "emphatically" supports the designation of wilderness for the islands, but is concerned that this would lead to a further erasing of the human history that has been so important in shaping the islands' ecosystems.[35] He argues:

> If visitors come here and believe they are experiencing pristine nature
> they will completely misunderstand not just the complex human
> history that has created the Apostle Islands of today; they will also fail
> to understand how much the natural ecosystems they encounter here
> have been shaped by that human history. In a very deep sense, what
> they will experience is not the natural and human reality of these is-
> lands, but a cultural myth that obscures much of what they most need

to understand about a wilderness that has long been a place of human dwelling.[36]

The difficulty lies in how we think about wilderness and how, subsequently, this becomes codified into law. The 1964 *Wilderness Act*, for example, identifies wilderness as a place where we humans are visitors only, leaving no trace of our incursions. But the Apostle Islands are far from being untouched by people: the Ojibwe lived for centuries here and European settlers since the 1800s lived on, fished from, farmed, logged (almost all of the islands had at some point been cleared), and built roads and homes here. The sharp dichotomy between us and the rest of nature inherent in the received wilderness idea means that designating something as wilderness is inconsistent with the maintenance of some of the obviously human-built artifacts, such as old buildings and roads, and certainly with educational signage. Calling a place "wilderness" seems to require, Cronon notes, our ability to remove all signs of prior human presence.[37]

However, Cronon complains, efforts to make, or remake, the islands into wilderness by removing or letting deteriorate the built structures, orchards, docks, roads, and the like, are not desirable. The human story, both Native and Euro-American, should not be hidden from visitors who seek wilderness. Historian James Feldman, in his detailed account of the interplay between humans and the islands, both before and since the wilderness designation, bluntly agrees that "removing or hiding the evidence does not change the past," even though much of the more significant human intervention ended decades ago.[38] Cronon believes, in fact, that signs should alert and educate people about that human history. The islands certainly look and feel like the wilderness of the received wilderness idea, at least to those unfamiliar with the ecology and human history of the area. But Cronon wants our experience of these places to be mediated not by the "cultural myth" in which human and wilderness history is separated, but by an awareness of the human stories of making the islands into what they are today.[39]

Cronon's solution to this tension is to employ the notion of "historical wilderness," which is a bit more consistent with the *Eastern Wilderness Act* of 1975 than the earlier, better known law. The 1975 legislation allows for designation of areas as wilderness that would not have counted as such under the original *Wilderness Act* due to evidence of mining, grazing, clear cutting, and the like, and grew out of the desire to be able to have wilderness areas east of the Rocky Mountains. But, Cronon observes, the National Parks Service generally applies a single policy emphasizing a sharp distinction between us and the rest of nature regarding structures, signage, and the like, regardless of whether the area was designated as wilderness according to the stricter 1964 or the looser 1975 act.[40] The two pieces of legislation do, though, indicate that there is room for diverse views regarding the human/nonhuman elements of wilderness. In Cronon's historical wilderness—where human and nonhuman stories are both valued— ecological restorations would not be allowed to remove all the evidence of human impacts; erasures would take place only when "absolutely necessary" and many of the structures would be actively preserved. The Apostle Islands' wilderness, Cronon concludes, should be thought of "as existing along a continuum, from areas that will be treated as 'pure' wilderness . . . to highly developed sites like the lighthouses that are managed almost entirely for nonwilderness values."[41]

PLURALISM AND THE IDEA OF WILDERNESS

Although Cronon's Apostle Islands case is quite removed from the serious problems of human welfare cited by Guha and Bayet, they are all part of the same issue: the received wilderness idea is malleable due to its socially constructed nature, which has allowed it to be shaped and used in ways more or less harmful. What is interesting about Cronon's solution of a historical wilderness, though, is that it demonstrates how, as Hacking had correctly noted, someone might point out the constructed nature of a concept in order to then suggest a reconceptualization. Callicott and Nelson do the same thing, suggesting solutions that focus our attention on the ecological (biodiversity reserves) and make us more aware of the pitfalls of ignoring our more mundane, lived-in places because we are misunderstanding wilderness.

Continuing, though, with Cronon's case for the moment, it might be objected that the historical wilderness notion changes the idea of wilderness too much. That is, it stretches the concept well beyond what any of us in this culture would count as wilderness. In fact, he wants us to overcome the dichotomy between us and the rest of nature in part by coming to see the Other in even our local spaces, conceptually shrinking the distance between wilderness and humanized place. He quotes Gary Snyder approvingly: "A person with a clear heart and open mind can experience the wilderness anywhere on earth"—even with a planted tree in a garden.[42] Waller balks at Cronon's (and by implication, Snyder's) move, saying that although the garden tree is in some senses "wild," it is markedly in a different situation, or context, than a tree in the forest; he notes, "if no boundaries exist between wild and tame, natural and unnatural, why shouldn't we establish parks to protect rock quarries, dammed rivers, and hog farms?"[43] Perhaps the problem in the Apostle Islands case is less with the idea of wilderness and more with a lack of alternative ways to protect places from further human-caused change. If we agree with Cronon to maintain structures and add interpretive signs, perhaps the Apostle Islands simply should not be called wilderness. This is certainly an option.

Nonetheless, Cronon's approach is attractive in that it loosens up the wilderness concept and, most significantly, mitigates to some serious extent the objection against the received view that it too starkly draws boundaries between us and the rest of nature. After all, this is the problem cited over and over in almost all of the objections to the wilderness idea. Without trying to draw here any lines regarding how much, or how obvious, or how ecologically negative any human-caused change to an area could be before it no longer is a candidate for wilderness, I do think that some expansion and revision of the concept is absolutely necessary in light of the rather successful deconstruction pursued by Cronon, Callicott and Nelson, and others. Once we have accepted as advantageous a certain flexibility in the concept, however, why not move further—not necessarily in terms of extending Cronon's continuum of less to more humanized place to count even more thoroughly humanized places as wilderness, but rather to embrace the concept of wilderness as involving a wider array of possible elements or images. There is nothing, after all, except potential inconsistencies of image and policy (e.g., how much management or how much human habitation, etc., is acceptable), that would prevent a widening—or to be clear, a *correction*—of the wilderness idea.

That there might be inconsistencies between the various notions of wilderness will undoubtedly bother us. It is essential that we figure out which models (e.g., biodiversity reserves, historical wilderness, etc.) can best avoid the problems of conceptual incoherence, lack of fit with other beliefs and values, and malignant practical effects—and which might aid us in our positive goals. But this does not mean that all the ways we think about wilderness must fit together in some seamless way. Pluralism can provide a useful framework.

The sort of pluralism that could prove useful here is drawn from the work of Martin Benjamin, who notes that "So long as individuals and groups enjoy a certain amount of freedom to think and act for themselves, there will be conflicts between good and important moral values and principles that cannot be resolved by reason."[44] Reasonable pluralism acknowledges that "a number of *good and important* ethical values and principles are inherently incompatible"—the implication being that there often is not a single, objectively correct view of things, but multiple reasonable possibilities.[45] This is different from a thoroughgoing relativism in which any view is just as good as any other. Pluralism requires that acceptable positions are defendable through reason rather than simply by whatever a group or individual happens to feel is right. We must be aware and on guard for biases, prejudices, and ignorance. Pluralism, so-understood, can provide a useful theoretical framework in which to understand wilderness since it allows for multiple, reasonable, but sometimes irreducibly conflicting beliefs about what wilderness is without succumbing to a problematic, anything-goes relativism.

The pluralism suggested here goes much further than Cronon's still unified model by being about not just variation in the extent of humanization allowable for a place to still be wilderness, but about conflicting metaphors or images of wilderness: what wilderness *means* to any one of us at any particular moment. That vision of wilderness changes, not merely in a linear, regressive or progressive way, but by shifting back and forth between, or involving at once, potentially conflicting and mutually irreducible conceptualizations that mediate our experience of both wilderness and our more mundane lives. For example, sometimes we think of nature as the Other, the habitat of nonhuman sentient experiencers, unconscious forces, raw materials for life and human betterment, or a place of worship. Sometimes we see and feel nature and wilderness as a place separate from us and sometimes we see it and ourselves as parts of the same whole; sometimes we dread, sometimes we are excited by, or drawn near to the Other; often we are ambivalent.

CONCLUSION

Fortunately, we are quite capable of simultaneously seeing the world from a variety of perspectives. Wilderness is not likely, to my mind, to be reduced to any a single notion—not a bio-reserve only or a historical wilderness only—but a set of sometimes inconsistent metaphors, models, and images. Any account of the social construction of wilderness, and hence of "wilderness" as a mediating concept, must take seriously this sort of pluralism. Because wilderness is a metaphor, or model—a conceptualization—there is no reason to insist that there is only one unifying meaning, even one that can be "stretched" one way or another (more humanized, less humanized) as needed. Although I cannot advance the argument further here, there seem to be several valuable but distinct notions of wilderness, some emphasizing the need for so-called mega-fauna to have space to flourish (Callicott's biodiversity reserves) and others honoring the people who shaped a place we now think of as wilderness (Cronon's historical wilderness). The possession of this set of meanings might well be superior to a single, unified image much the way that working with competing and incommensurable models in science can be more fruitful than insisting on a single model, paradigm, or metaphor.

In fact, because these are competing metaphors and images, and not subject only to rational argumentation, it makes little sense to defend any particular notion of wilderness as the ultimate, singly correct vision. But at the same time, each must be subject to critical appraisal, as we saw with the received wilderness idea. Pluralism—which fits neatly with the critical realist position regarding social construction—tacks between flexibility and the conviction that conceptualizations are nonetheless open to thoughtful criticism and reformation. Successful ideas must be as coherent as is possible, or as reasonable as can be given the complexity of the world and our limited ability to neutrally evaluate. Further, they must fit with our other beliefs about ourselves and the world, and must not lead to unnecessary bad or immoral consequences.

Reconstructing deconstructed notions need not be an exercise in getting a concept fixed and purified so we can then forget that this too is a conceptualization of something. I expect that wilderness as a core Western concept will not disappear anytime soon, and in fact, it will likely continue to involve a variety of inconsistent notions. But I do believe that the received wilderness idea can be freed of many of its more sinister problems and consequences, though alternatives will all be limited in their own ways. Further, as James Morton Turner concludes in *The Promise of Wilderness: American Environmental Politics since 1964*, "Wilderness protection has provided an immediate, tangible, and positive goal for environmental advocates. . . . Creating a wilderness area protects a discrete place. You can locate a wilderness area on a map, you can drive to an overlook and look out at protected peaks and valleys, you can hike into it, and you can share it."[46] The wilderness idea is pragmatically and ecologically powerful because it is emotionally powerful, even if it is too limited to serve as the cornerstone of environmental policy moving forward. Callicott and Nelson, Cronon, and other critics are right to push us beyond uncritically accepting the concept as we have inherited it, but yet people should and will continue reading the literature, viewing the art, and embracing the poetry implicated in the development of the problematic historical notion of wilderness. We should not turn our backs and ignore our social and intellectual history, nor should we ignore the potential wilderness has as an idea in the continued efforts to forge a better relationship with the rest of the world. The solution can only be that people understand wilderness for what it is—both a place and a variety of particular ways in which we, in our particular time and culture, see ourselves and less-humanized nature.

JASON MATZKE, professor of philosophy at the University of Mary Washington, teaches environmental and medical ethics, social and political philosophy, ethical theory, and philosophy of law.

NOTES

1. René Descartes, *Meditations on First Philosophy*, trans. Donald A. Cress (Indianapolis: Hackett Publishing, 1993), 22. Descartes notes: "what I thought I had seen with my eyes, I actually grasped solely with the faculty of judgment, which is in my mind" (22).

2. John Locke, *An Essay Concerning Human Understanding*, ed. A. D. Wozley (New York: Meridian, Penguin Book, 1964), 112–19.

3. Ramachandra Guha, "Radical American Environmentalism and Wilderness Preservation: A Third World Critique," in *The Great New Wilderness Debate*, ed. J. Baird Callicott and Michael Nelson (Athens: University of Georgia Press, 1998), 235.

4. J. Baird Callicott and Michael Nelson, "Introduction," in *The Great New Wilderness Debate*, ed. J. Baird Callicott and Michael Nelson (Athens: University of Georgia Press, 1998), 2, 4, and 6.

5. Much of the discussion regarding the changing meaning of concepts such as "wilderness" and "nature" proceeds without much (or any) analysis of these three questions. This is true, for example, even of the award-winning book by Andrea Wulf entitled *The Invention of Nature: Alexander von Humboldt's New World* (New York: Vintage Books, 2015); see also Caitlin Finlayson's review in this issue of *Environment, Space, Place*. Mark Harvey's detailed biography of Howard Zahniser, wilderness advocate and key author of the 1964 *Wilderness Act*, is similarly (and quite reasonably) more about the man and his influence than about the philosophical difficulties raised by Guha, Callicott and Nelson, Cronon, and the like (*Wilderness Forever: Howard Zahniser and the Path to the Wilderness Act* [Seattle: University of Washington Press, 2005]). Douglas Brinkley's masterful *The Wilderness Warrior: Theodore Roosevelt and the Crusade for America* is similarly an important contribution for anyone seeking to better understand the evolution of the wilderness notion and its impact, but it leaves (again, without fault) the philosophical questions for another day (New York: Harper Perennial, 2009).

6. William Cronon, "The Trouble with Wilderness; or, Getting Back to the Wrong Nature," in *Uncommon Ground: Rethinking the Human Place in Nature*, ed. William Cronon (New York: Norton, 1996), 69–70.

7. Ibid, 70.

8. Ibid, 81 (emphasis in original).

9. Ian Hacking, *The Social Construction of What?* (Cambridge, Mass.: Harvard University Press, 1999), 6 and 12.

10. Cronon, "The Trouble with Wilderness," 70–73.

11. Callicott and Nelson, "Introduction," 4–5.

12. William Cronon, "Foreword to the Paperback Edition," in *Uncommon Ground: Rethinking the Human Place in Nature*, ed. William Cronon (New York: Norton, 1996), 21.

13. Dave Foreman, "Wilderness Areas for Real," in *The Great New Wilderness Debate*, ed. J. Baird Callicott and Michael Nelson (Athens: University of Georgia Press, 1998), 396.

14. Cronon, "Foreword," 21.

15. Cronon, "The Trouble with Wilderness," 70.

16. J. Baird Callicott, "Should Wilderness Areas Become Biodiversity Reserves?," in *The*

Great New Wilderness Debate, ed. J. Baird Callicott and Michael Nelson (Athens: University of Georgia Press, 1998), 587 (emphasis in original).

17. Hacking, 6, 12.
18. Callicott and Nelson, "Introduction," 2 and 12.
19. J. Baird Callicott, "The Wilderness Idea Revisited: The Sustainable Development Alternative," in *The Great New Wilderness Debate*, ed. J. Baird Callicott and Michael Nelson (Athens: University of Georgia Press, 1998), 349.
20. Ibid, 348 and 350.
21. Cronon, "The Trouble with Wilderness, 80–81.
22. Ibid, 79.
23. Donald Waller, "Getting back to the Right Nature: A Reply to Cronon's 'The Trouble with Wilderness," in *The Great New Wilderness Debate*, ed. J. Baird Callicott and Michael Nelson (Athens: University of Georgia Press, 1998), 554.
24. Reed Noss, "Sustainability and Wilderness," in *The Great New Wilderness Debate*, ed. J. Baird Callicott and Michael Nelson (Athens: University of Georgia Press, 1998), 409.
25. Callicott, "The Wilderness Idea Revisited," 350–51.
26. Val Plumwood, "Wilderness Skepticism and Wilderness Dualism," in *The Great New Wilderness Debate*, ed. J. Baird Callicott and Michael Nelson (Athens: University of Georgia Press, 1998), 669.
27. William Denevan, "The Pristine Myth: The Landscape of the Americas in 1492," in *The Great New Wilderness Debate*, ed. J. Baird Callicott and Michael Nelson (Athens: University of Georgia Press, 1998), 415–17.
28. Ibid, 417.
29. Callicott, "The Wilderness Idea Revisited," 348.
30. Cronon, "The Trouble with Wilderness," 85.
31. Guha, "Radical American Environmentalism," 232.
32. Ibid, 235; and Ramachandra Guha, "Deep Ecology Revisited," in *The Great New Wilderness Debate*, ed. J. Baird Callicott and Michael Nelson (Athens: University of Georgia Press, 1998), 277.
33. Fabienne Bayet, "Overturning the Doctrine: Indigenous People and Wilderness— Being Aboriginal in the Environmental Movement," in *The Great New Wilderness Debate*, ed. J. Baird Callicott and Michael Nelson (Athens: University of Georgia Press, 1998), 314 and 318.
34. Callicott and Nelson, "Introduction," 13.
35. William Cronon, "The Riddle of the Apostle Islands: How do you manage a wilderness full of human stories?" *Orion* 22, no. 3 (2003): 38. For more on how the various federal agencies responsible for wilderness actually do manage such areas, see Randall Wilson's "National Wilderness Preservation System," a chapter in his monograph *America's Public Lands: From Yellowstone to Smokey Bear and Beyond* (Lanham, Md.: Rowman & Littlefield, 2014), 219–53.
36. William Cronon, "The Riddle of the Apostle Islands," 38.
37. Ibid, 36, 38, and 39. Cronon also points us to a similar story and set of problems as told by environmental historian Laura Alice Watt in her fascinating volume *The Paradox of Preservation: Wilderness and Working Landscapes at Point Reyes National Seashore* (Oakland: University of California Press, 2017). Samuel MacDonald's *The*

Agony of an American Wilderness: Loggers, Environmentalists, and the Struggle for Control of a Forgotten Forest, tells a slightly different story in that he focuses mostly on the struggles and conflicts between people who have very different interests and perspectives regarding managing an area greatly changed by human industry but with some potential wilderness; his book is also nonetheless important in its illustration of the difficulties that are imbedded in our conceptualizations of "natural" vs. humanized lands (Lanham, Md.: Rowman & Littlefield, 2005).

38. James Feldman, *A Storied Wilderness: Rewilding the Apostle Islands* (Seattle: University of Washington Press, 2011), 217. Feldman points out that few would today question the wild character of much of the Islands since "more than one hundred years have passed since the last quarrying, more than sixty years since the last farming, and more than thirty years since the last logging" (218).
39. Cronon, "The Riddle of the Apostle Islands," 38.
40. Ibid, 39.
41. Ibid, 41 and 42.
42. Cronon, "The Trouble with Wilderness," 88–89.
43. Waller, "Getting back to the Right Nature," 544–45.
44. Martin Benjamin, *Philosophy and this Actual World* (Lanham, Md.: Rowman & Littlefield Publishers, 2003), 124.
45. Ibid, 125–27 (emphasis in original).
46. James Morton Turner, *The Promise of Wilderness: American Environmental Politics since 1964* (Seattle: University of Washington Press, 2012), 396.

A Perception of Environment from a Floating-land

Unearthing an Apposite Term

KALPITA BHAR PAUL

Abstract

Insights from phenomenological narratives of environmental change, led me to inquire on how to capture the dynamicity and relational reality of the Sundarbans's environment, as articulated by the islanders. Existing concepts to represent one's surroundings, I argue, have their own limitations and I propose the term saṃsāra *from Indian philosophy as an alternative. I contend that the hermeneutic of* saṃsāra *could craft out a new dimension of the concept and thus could very well capture the experience of the islanders. The hermeneutic of* saṃsāra *and its translation to English, teases out deeper phenomenological nuances of the human—environment relationship. I also demonstrate the implications of this conceptualization in the literature of ecophenomenology and advocate that the notion of* saṃsāra *illuminates some of the key features of the human—environment relationship, which till now were not duly acknowledged in this literature.*

INTRODUCTION

The Sundarbans, the world largest single block halophytic mangrove forest spreads in India and Bangladesh, has become a global concern in the era of climate crisis due to its vulnerability to climate change. The Sundarbans is a cluster of islands that have been formed by river Ganga, Padma, and Brahmaputra. Over the last decade, several WWF (World Wild Foundation), CSE (Centre for Science and Environment), or even IPCC (Intergovernmental Panel on Climate Change) reports have repeatedly pointed out the increasing vulnerability of the Sundarbans ecoregion to climate change. The world-wide predictions of increased frequency of various natural calamities, have made the Sundarbans a point of global concern as this really magnificent mangrove forest fosters rich biodiversity that includes some charismatic species as well.[1] Not only that, the Indian Sundarbans region consists of 102 islands, and fifty-four of which are heavily populated with human settlements.[2] In this context, on one hand, the Sundarbans being an ecoregion and a biodiversity hotspot of India has widely attracted attention of ecologists to protect it from climate change and to save its biodiversity; on the other, to safeguard the human settlements from natural calamities like flood, cyclone, there is a constant drive for so-called developmental activities that can perhaps enable the islanders to cope with various environmental changes these islands are presently witnessing or going to face in the near future. To protect and conserve biodiversity of these islands as well as the human settlements, numerous projects are currently being implemented in the Sundarbans.

By acknowledging the vulnerability of the Sundarbans's environment, this essay will explore the phenomenological understanding of what is the meaning of environment for the inhabitants who dwell in these islands and witness numerous changes in land and the environment, in their everyday life. I demonstrate that the phenomenological experience of the Sundarbans's environment offers a distinct realization, starkly different from the conventional notion of environment. Islanders' narratives accentuate the relationship between an individual and the environment, rather than focusing on the environment being a separate entity. I borrow the Indian philosophical concept of *saṃsāra* and argue that a hermeneutical analysis of *saṃsāra* has the potential to capture the nuances of the human—environment relationship, as perceived in these islands. This analysis, I posit, will bring some fresh insights in the discourse of the Sundarbans's protection and conservation, and will demonstrate the need to uphold the true essence of the Sundarbans's environment. I will also make an attempt to translate the concept *saṃsāra* to find an equivalent English term that can capture the similar sense of the human—environment relationship. For this, I will borrow the concept of "world" from the discipline of phenomenology and will demonstrate that the concept of "phenomenological world" is capable of capturing the notion of *saṃsāra* in English. Subsequently, I will also exhibit how this conceptualization of the human—environment relationship can contribute to the broader discourse of ecophenomenology.

PHENOMENOLOGY OF THE SUNDARBANS' ENVIRONMENT: VOICE OF THE DWELLERS

Taking all the geological features of the Sundarbans into consideration, I have chosen the G-plot island to conduct a field study. I have employed Interpretive Phenomenological Research methodology to capture the everyday experiences of these islanders.[3] Here, I will provide some excerpts from these phenomenological narratives to demonstrate the islander's distinct relation to the environment. From these narratives, one could derive that the narrators have mentioned about the dynamicity of environmental entities and the relational existence of environment in reference to their day-to-day experiences. While describing environmental changes of that region, these unique features associated with their conception of environment, repeatedly get reflected in their voices.

During my field study in the island, I have collected phenomenological narratives of twenty-seven individuals across age, gender, and livelihoods. Almost all of the narrators have articulated a similar notion of environment from their varied contexts. In the following, I provide a few excerpts of those narratives among which the first three denote the dynamicity of the environment as articulated by the narrators, and the last three presents the relational reality as perceived by the islanders:

> Now there is a huge sand dune on the river-bund of south G-plot. However, no one can ensure anything, maybe within a day, this sand dune will get completely abolished. It is just like a magic. It is difficult to assume how the river will flow.[4]

> Water cannot grasp the entire land, there will always be some land for us to live. I know may be after one or two more floods, I cannot stay here. This house is going to go. But new shore land is coming up, that portion of the land perhaps will be there for us to settle down. This island was not like that forever, it is always changing its size and shape, nothing is fixed here.[5]

> Easterly wind is the most dangerous one. Commonly, we know that during spring tides the water will be full till embankment, and the

river will go far away during neap tides. But no one can ensure anything, easterly wind becomes the deciding factor. Two major floods,
82's flood and 2010's Aila, nevertheless, did not occur during spring
tide. These occurred during neap tide when water level remains
usually very low. In this kind of situations, easterly wind becomes
the deciding element, so we call it "the king."[6]

Outsiders ask why we stay so close to the river. But in this area, it is
actually safer to stay near the river, areas far from the river can easily
get water locked. There are no high land and low land in this area, land
is land until the water takes over it.[7]

I cannot count the number of times in a day I go to the river. The river
is just beside; even you can say that the land of this house also a few
years back was the river. . . . During the low-pressure time, the sound
of the river waves is so alarming that you would think that the river is
going to grasp you.[8]

As a resident of the Sundarbans, flood is not a new phenomenon for
us. It is not something that we feel scared of. During floods, we will
not get food, we cannot do farming—that's all, but no one will die due
to that. The tide will bring the flood and after that during ebb water
will drain out—that is the feature of this river-bounded place. It is like
those red crabs that stay at the beaches. Whenever the tide comes they
go deep into sand holes, again come out during ebb. People in G-plot
live exactly like that.[9]

What does it mean to be in the midst of the environment? The residents
of the G-plot, as per their geographic location, live their life surrounded
by rivers and the Bay of Bengal. Massive distance from the mainland
separates the islanders and makes them feel confined within the water
boundary. Living a life by accepting these realities always seems chal-
lenging from an outsider's perspective. The above narratives, however,
clearly depict that the way islanders conceptualize the environment is
quite different from the outsider's conception of it and thus, there is a
difference between insider's and outsider's perceptions of the Sundarbans. These narratives illustrate that the islanders are not afraid of the

changing features of the environment, neither it is a new phenomenon for them. Their experiences clearly vindicate that for them the Sundarbans is a place where changes in the surroundings are a constant feature of the place and inhabitant of this place live in-tune with it. Precisely for this reason, the islanders' engagements with their surroundings shape how these changing features of the Sundarbans are going to appear to one.

To illuminate the cause behind the difference between insider's and outsider's perceptions, Tuan argues how experiences play an important role to make a place a center of meaning.[10] Tuan elaborates that narratives help to grasp a place that is "deeply humanized world"[11] and narratives also explicate how experiences turn a place into a center of meaning. He says, "Outsiders say 'nature,' because the environment seems barely touched. Insiders see 'homeplace'—an environment that is familiar to them, not because they have materially transformed it but because they have named it. It is their place—their world—through the casting of a linguistic net."[12] In this regard, the aforementioned experiential accounts of the islanders could guide us to grasp the embodied experience of the Sundarbans's environment. These also demonstrate, for the islanders, the "homeplace" Sundarbans becomes a center of meaning through their experiential understanding of their surroundings.[13] A close-reading of the narratives shows that there is hardly any static conception of the environment in this region, instead they preserve a unique conception of the Sundarbans's environment. This unique conception of their surroundings on one hand, holds the dynamicity of the environmental entity, on the other hand, elucidates the relational existence of the environment. For the narrators, the environment is not only an aggregation of biotic and abiotic components. The dynamic and the relational presence of the surroundings are the essence of their understanding of it. Living a life in the midst of the environment enables them to appreciate the dynamicity and its relational existence. Therefore, I posit, it is necessary to evaluate how far the current available terms in English as well as in Bengali[14] can capture these subtle nuances or how far these nuances commensurate well with the existing terms which define one's surroundings. This inquiry will prove to be beneficial in finding an apposite term. This is particularly required as without grasping all these articulated nuances, we would fail to understand what environment is for the people of the Sundarbans and how they conceptualize the vulnerability of the Sundarbans.

THE EXISTING TERMS: A BRIEF ANALYSIS

The first term, which comes to mind, for denoting one's surroundings is environment. As per etymological roots, the word "environment" has been derived from the word "environ." Environ means what is surrounding us. Extending the word environ, environment denotes "state of being environed."[15] The word environment precisely defines the condition in which a person or a thing lives or is placed. From this point of view, environment is nothing but the aggregation of the components which are environing us. Similarly, the Bengali word *paribesh*, a common translation of environment, can also be traced back to the word *paribeston*—the translation of "environ." Following that, *paribesh* can be considered as the word that aptly describes the components that surrounds us. Thus, both the words, environment and *paribesh*, describe the elements and the surroundings within which an individual is placed in. These terminologies, however, neither capture the dynamicity nor the relational reality of their surroundings as depicted in the narratives. Instead, these terms seem to indicate a certain static condition, a stable outside that sustains human and other things inside.

In this regard, one obvious suggestion could be to use the word ecology, as it is also a widely-accepted word that can denote the surroundings of an individual. The word ecology defines the study (logy) of habitat (eco). Instead of asking what is environment if one asks what is ecology, it precisely explains the "relationship of living things to their environment."[16] Marshall emphasizes that ecology and its major concepts to grasp the natural world deal with organisms and their environment as an integrated whole.[17] Ecology puts a special emphasis on living entities and studies how a living entity relates to non-living things as well as other living entities. In this manner, ecology as a term focuses on the relational existence. In Bengali vocabulary, ecology has been translated as *bastabya bidya*. In Bengali, *bastabya* originates from the word *bastu* which denotes the dwelling place and *bidya* refers to knowledge. Following that, *bastu bidya* literally refers to knowledge about the place of dwelling. As a translation of ecology, *bastabya bidya* also refers to the knowledge about the relationship between living entities with their environment. *Bastabya bidya*, however, as a translation of ecology remains rather confined to textual references. Whereas, in common usage of this term in Bengali, *bastu bidya* or *bastu shastra* refers to the traditional Hindu system of designing architecture in such a way that a building follows the law of nature and becomes an ideal place for inhabitation. One can find very restricted usage of the word indicating ecology, and more often, it is commonly used to refer to the knowledge of housing or architecture. Hence, on one hand, though ecology as a word according to English dictionary is capable of capturing the relational existence of human beings and the environment, it falls short to grasp the dynamicity in the surroundings, mentioned by the narrators. On the other hand, the translation of ecology in Bengali is quite limited to textual references and its common usage fails to capture the semantic space of the word ecology.

At this juncture, one might evoke the term nature as a possible one for serving the purpose. First of all, this term is loaded with various definitions and has often been overused in different discourses. Secondly, nature, generally, points towards a transcendental realm and refers to the cosmological order. For both of these reasons, nature becomes a problematic term to refer to.[18] In Bengali, the translation of nature is either *prakriti* or *nisarga*. Both the words point towards some supreme realm which is transcendental. I found quite often the narrators equate *prakriti* with the universe. Here, one could say that nature offers a sense of eternity and holistic existence. The common notion about nature or *prakriti* is that it is unfathomable. And thus, it is commonly equated with the super realm or God. Hence, I consciously refrain myself from delegating the word nature or its Bengali equivalents as the appropriate terms that can represent the notion of surroundings as depicted by the narrators.

The thorough examination of the most commonly used terms—environment, ecology and nature, as well as their translation in Bengali—reveals that these fall short to capture the nuances present in the islanders' descriptions of their surroundings. In this regard, a frequently referred Bengali term by the narrators comes to my mind, which is *saṃsāra*. Here, I would like to clarify that the narrators have not really used the term *saṃsāra* to denote their surroundings. Rather, the word *saṃsāra* has a very different connotation in its colloquial usage in Bengali, and I will elaborate that in the next section. Despite this divergence, I argue that the word *saṃsāra* can still be a potential term to capture the islanders' perception of their surroundings.

Saṃsāra, on one hand, is a well-known concept in Indian philosophy having its own connotations. On the other hand, *saṃsāra*[19] as a Bengali word possesses quite a different notion that does not match with its philosophical concept. These two distinct connotations of *saṃsāra* indicate the incongruity between its theoretical understanding and colloquial usage. Instead, keeping these two usages distinctly separate from each other and preserving this as a static concept or dead one, I vouch, a phenomenological understanding of the *saṃsāra* could effectively establish a communication between its two articulations and make it a living concept. To make the concept alive, I will carry out a hermeneutic analysis of *saṃsāra*. This will help in extending its semantic space to plausibly capture the perceptions of the islanders.

HERMENEUTIC OF THE CONCEPT OF SAṂSĀRA

To carry out this hermeneutic, first of all, I borrow the methodology from Cameron (2014).[20] Cameron extends Gadamer's hermeneutics, which reveals the connection between language and the world, in the context of environmental hermeneutics.[21] He points out that the creation of a concept is based on receiving feedback from worldly experiences. Once a concept gets created, it gets embedded in the language and subsequently, begins to structure our experiences. Furthermore, Cameron highlights that Gadamer critiques the human nature of hypostatizing world and concepts as it creates illusions. Pertaining to this nature of hypostatization, human beings are prone to refrain themselves from critically scrutinizing expectations that are conceptually constituted to comprehend the world. Consequently, a disappointment might arise due to the divergence between expectations and real-world experiences. A thorough evaluation of this disappointment can bring forth a shift in the expectation by extending or reinterpreting the concept while taking account of our actual worldly experiences. Otherwise, the concept remains the same and the disappointment persists.

In this regard, Cameron elaborates that Gadamer proposes to transcend this illusion by "revealing the continuous, dynamic, historical, and hermeneutic interaction of concept and world in concrete experiences."[22] Borrowing from Gadamer, Cameron also emphasizes that the relationship between concepts and the world is a dynamic one, and he explains it through the three step hermeneutic process. Following that process, I will try to offer a hermeneutic of the concept "*saṃsāra*" to show how this can capture the narrators' sense of the surroundings as a dynamic as well as a relational reality.

The first step is to explore the "inherited presupposition" about a concept. In the Upanishad, around 600BC, the term *saṃsāra* can be traced to have first appeared.[23] *Saṃsāra* is basically a Sanskrit word, and in Indian philosophy, the concept *saṃsāra* comes along with the concepts of nirvāṇa and the cycle of birth and rebirth. In Indian philosophy, the world is considered as the only reality, however, the world is experienced in two different ways, *saṃsāra* and nirvāṇa. *Saṃsāra* is the relative world that is experienced by each and every individual differently. Here, one could possibly ask what does this "relative world" indicate? Relative world is the experience in which, an individual from a first person point of view, distinctly perceives the world as an aggregation of objects that interact causally in space and time.[24] According to its conception, *saṃsāra* is the dependent world that appears differently to each individual. As indicated, it is the opposite of another kind of experience of the world, nirvāṇa. Nirvāṇa is the world that transcends any kind of dependence. It denotes the world in its true form.

In this regard, as I have mentioned, *saṃsāra* is intricately connected with the concept of cycle of birth and rebirth. The traditional Indian philosophical thought indicates that avidyā (ignorance) is the root cause due to which an individual remains trapped in the cycle of birth and rebirth. Because of ignorance or avidyā, an individual gets engrossed in her everyday world and that eventually leads her to create this dependent world or *saṃsāra*. Avidyā bounds one to remain trapped in the samsaric realm. Ryan clearly points out that avidyā drives karma (action) and becomes the deciding factor in determining whether it will be possible for an individual to transcend this realm of the dependent world or to go beyond *saṃsāra* to attain nirvāṇa or not.[25] In the same vein, avidyā stimulates craving, conceptualizing, and causality, and as per Loy[26] these three factors together decide whether one can go beyond the realm of *saṃsāra* to attain nirvāṇa or not. However, here, it is more important to highlight that whatever the reason might be, *saṃsāra* in its Indian philosophical conceptualization denotes a relational reality of the world which comprises of all the attributes that impede one to attain nirvāṇa and therefore, it is considered as an obnoxious realm to dwell in. Owing to different reasons, as put forth by various traditions, an individual fails to realize the ultimate reality of the world and falls back into this wheel of *saṃsāra*, which is the cycle of birth and rebirth.

Furthermore, as per Indian philosophical traditions, the main characteristic of *saṃsāra* is suffering. The concept of suffering illustrates how suffering or *duḥkha* leads one to dwell within the cycle of birth and rebirth and eventually the individual remains caught in the *saṃsāra*. Matilal in his essay, "Duhkha, Nirvana, and Holy Men," describes life experience of human beings in the realm of *saṃsāra* is equivalent to pain and anguish.[27] He shows how pain or *duḥkha* or suffering becomes the central issue of the Indian philosophical schools. These schools demonstrate that "our earthly existence, our profane life, our everyday routine, is not to be regarded as final."[28] Indeed, Indian philosophy attempts to establish that there is a sacred existence which is beyond this mundane one, for human beings to attain to. To attain this sacred existence, one needs to overcome *duḥkha* or needs to transcend the samsaric realm. In the realm of *saṃsāra*, as Matilal would say, the human existence is caught up in a conditioned state where one cannot access her free will, though we are seen as free agents; whereas, nirvāṇa is an "unconditioned state of freedom."[29] Until one manages to comprehend *avidyā* and its consequence as *duḥkha*, the individual would remain caught in the cyclic order of birth and rebirth in *saṃsāra* and thereby would fail to attain nirvāṇa. Thus, *saṃsāra* in Indian philosophy, becomes the repetitive occurrence of life events, which Danto has mentioned as "despair of life."[30] Danto further claims that this despair of life makes Indian philosophy to promote the need to endeavor for moksha or nirvāṇa or otherworldly lives. Hence, it can be concluded that where nirvāṇa is a blissful experience of the human existence and a transcendental reality of human's free will or unconditioned existence, *saṃsāra* comprises of the everyday reality encumbered with *duḥkha* or pain.

In his second step, Cameron shows how Gadamer includes phenomenological reflection to explain the relation between the world and the concept.[31] In Bengali vocabulary, *saṃsāra* is quite a common term and usually denotes family affairs arising in day-to-day life. The philosophical concept of *saṃsāra* and its negative undertone, however, do not prevalently exist in its common usage. I think it is worth exploring the common usage of *saṃsāra*, as derived from the phenomenological experience, to find out the divergence between its theoretical expectation and colloquial usage.

Commonly, individuals refer to the word *saṃsāra* to express their relationships, liabilities, and the constant need for adapting to changing circumstances. Not only the proximate relationship, but people also refer to a distant relationship or a universal connection with other human and non-human beings by the term *jagat saṃsāra*—where *jagat* represents the universe and "*saṃsāra*" literally denotes family. During general conversations with the islanders, many of them often invoked the idea that "*Saṃsāra* is a play or a drama." No one has a choice to decide whether to partake in this samsaric realm; rather everyone by default is an actor of that play. The word is also attached with the connotation that in *saṃsāra*, pain and pleasure comes in a cyclic order and nothing is permanent in it. Therefore, everyone will experience pain as well as pleasure, or happiness and sorrow. In Bengali, the proverb "*Sukh Duhkha Pala Kore Ase*" also means the same, joy and sorrow come in turn. Through this notion of cyclic order, *saṃsāra* creates a "cyclic world" where nothing is static or permanent, and it also points to the repetitive occurrence of life events. In this way, the term *saṃsāra* is capable of signifying the dynamicity of our lives. Here, I would like to posit that where life is intricately connected to one's surroundings and where the dynamicity of life and the dynamicity of surroundings do not remain distinctly separate from each other, the term *saṃsāra* is equally capable of capturing the notion of dynamicity of one's surroundings.

Furthermore, in its common usage, *saṃsāra* refers to the mundane existence. It denotes the relationship of every individual with other human beings and lifeforms. Another proverb that I would like to mention in this regard is: "the family is like a forest: if you are outside, it is dense; if you are inside, you see that each tree has its own position." In this proverb, family actually refers to *saṃsāra*, and the proverb tries to communicate that though from the outset, the samsaric realm seems complex and full of liabilities, from the inside, one can realize that an individual or an entity in the *saṃsāra* has one's own demarcated position and clearly defined responsibilities. One's position and responsibilities actually define one's association with others. That is how for each individual, *saṃsāra* manifests differently. In this manner, *saṃsāra* also echoes the concept of a relative world, where the world is experienced by each individual differently. By considering this articulation of *saṃsāra*, one could argue that there are subtle but definite differences between *saṃsāra* as a philosophical concept and *saṃsāra* as a phenomenological experience. In an everyday world, the phenomenological experience of *saṃsāra* and its articulation elucidate that the experience of *saṃsāra* is not same for everyone, every individual creates one's own *saṃsāra* through one's relationship with other human beings, lifeforms, and other worldly entities. Thus, for each of us, *saṃsāra* refers to certain relationships, entities, responsibilities, and emotive experiences, but it hardly has any covert negative undertone like its philosophical conceptualization. This articulation and understanding of *saṃsāra* take us to Cameron's argument that this subtle difference between experiences and concept can induce a disappointment.

The disappointment between this "inherited presupposition" and experience leads to the third step where borrowing from Gadamer, Cameron argues against the hypostatization of any concept. Instead of carrying a concept just like a dead one, it is necessary to reconstitute it by taking account of the disjunction between the concept and experiences. The disappointment emerged from experiences, therefore, leads towards the reinterpretation of the concept. This dynamic relationship between a concept and the worldly experiences can only make a concept a living one. At this juncture, a reinterpretation of the concept *saṃsāra*, is necessary. As discussed above, *saṃsāra* as a philosophical concept defines a realm where everyone suffers and remains trapped, however, the phenomenological experience of *saṃsāra* indicates human life and life events, the relational reality of each person amid various living and non-living entities. It also shows that how a change in outside, can induce a change in one's inside. This, in a way, illuminates one of the fundamental truths of life, which is change; as one Bengali proverb, "*Paribartan e jiboner niyom*," (Change is the norm of life) denotes exactly the same sense. Thus, the dynamicity of outside as well as inside drives our lives and the realm of *saṃsāra*. Here, I think, it would not be wrong to argue that, in this sense, *saṃsāra* indeed a relational reality to one's surroundings which constantly gets modified by outer changes and inner motives. I would like to elaborate on this from an example of the Sundarbans islanders' narratives. Post Aila, there was an upsurge in soil salinity and due to that cultivation or per se any agricultural activities became impossible for a few years in this region. In that period, islanders have changed farm lands into salt water ponds for fishing. With this transition, a farmer becomes a fish cultivator and for that matter one's relation to his/her surroundings gets altered. Thus, the dynamicity of outside induces changes inside and drives our lives in the realm of *saṃsāra*. Hence, I posit, *saṃsāra* appropriately provides the opportunity to grasp the perspectives that are articulated by the narrators. In the everyday world, our relationships with our surroundings are actually like dwelling in *saṃsāra*. Human beings with very special attributes create the relational reality of saṃsāra. In this manner, the realm of *saṃsāra* has a very special association to each one of us according to one's own lived-experiences. Therefore, I see, introducing the concept *saṃsāra* to articulate and comprehend the dynamic and relational reality of our surroundings, will not be a futile attempt.

REDEFINING THE NOTION OF SAṂSĀRA

The disjunction between philosophical concept and everyday usage of *saṃsāra* demonstrates that the phenomenological experience of *saṃsāra* does not talk about a realm incumbent with sorrow and pain as conceptualized in its philosophical concept, however, it emphasizes a cyclic occurrence of life-events similar to its philosophical conceptualization. Moreover, it also highlights the occurrence of change in one's relation to the surroundings due to changing affairs without any covert negative undertone. This understanding encourages me to introduce *saṃsāra*, instead of environment, ecology, or nature, as a term to put forth one's relation to one's surroundings. It also offers a notion that each individual creates a special relation to her surroundings depending on her life course. *Saṃsāra* depicts that both the life of an individual and her surroundings go through several changes as there is nothing permanent as such in *saṃsāra*. The acceptance of the term *saṃsāra* helps to go beyond the idea of a stable surroundings and in turn, promotes that one's dwelling in *saṃsāra* must be in tandem with its changing surroundings, instead of intervening or curbing any changes occurring in it. Along with these, it also points out the inherent possibility of altering one's relation to the surroundings and other beings. Hence, I argue, accepting the term *saṃsāra* could offer a new way to comprehend the human—environment relationship. In this regard, it is necessary to clarify that *saṃsāra* precisely captures the deeper nuances of the human—environment relationship instead of just capturing a notion of the physical world, independent of the presence of human beings. The islanders' descriptions succinctly depict how an individual is always at the center of *saṃsāra* or in other words how without the presence of human beings the realm of *saṃsāra* would fall apart. In this manner, I think, *saṃsāra* helps to phenomenologically approach the relationship rather than getting caught into the theoretical understanding of environment and ecology. In one line, it can be concluded that *saṃsāra* is a term that defines the phenomenological relationship of an individual to her surroundings.

KEEPING THE CONCEPT ALIVE: TRANSLATION OF SAṂSĀRA

If one accepts that *saṃsāra* could be an apt term to denote the surroundings where human beings are emplaced into, then the next question arises what would be an appropriate term to capture this notion of *saṃsāra* in English. One convenient way to go about it is to transliterate the term *saṃsāra*. In this case, the limitation of transliteration, as Sarukkai underlines, is it limits the scope of modifying a concept in the translated language and the concept again becomes a dead one, and consequently, the process of transmission and circulation gets restricted.[32] Hence, Sarukkai argues the transliterated concept remains an "alien concept" for the translated language. In this context, Sarukkai emphasizes the differences between translation of a concept and translation of a word. He mentions that for translating a concept, it is important to comprehend the concept in a new language with its "meaning-bearing capacity."[33] He urges to take account of the context to comprehend a concept rather than just to find an equivalent word.

While translating a concept, translation works as a method through which the concept gets translated along with its context to entirely retain its meaning-bearing capacity.

Translation as a method is an appropriate way of translating any alien concepts, like *saṃsāra*. The primary characteristic of an alien concepts is these are "foreign to the conceptual structure that informs cognitive capacities of different communities."[34] In other words, alien concepts can have varied meaning for a particular community. On one hand, the philosophical conceptualization of *saṃsāra* clearly differs from its meanings in everyday usage. On the other hand, *saṃsāra* does not get acknowledged as a term for articulating the notion of the environment. Hence, this alien concept needs to be translated carefully by keeping the fact in mind that accepting *saṃsāra* as a translation of the notion of environment does not imply that these two are same, instead, it emphasizes that there is a need to extend the boundaries of both the concepts. According to Sarukkai, ambiguous initial engagements to grapple with an alien concept, can slowly make the concept a familiar one and over time, extends its semantic space.

Considering the phenomenological understanding of *saṃsāra*, I posit, the concept of "world" in phenomenology or "phenomenological world" could be a plausible translation of *saṃsāra*. The concept of "phenomenological world" has a distinct connotation in the English language as it originates from the Western philosophical stream of phenomenology. At the outset, I would like to clarify that, here, I borrow the concept of world from Heidegger's phenomenology instead of Husserl's. In his magnum opus, Heidegger strictly negates Husserl's phenomenological methodology[35] and introduces his phenomenology as a hermeneutical or interpretive understanding of the world.[36] Heidegger readily negates the possibility of mere description of sense data. Indeed, instead of bumping into an object and describing it, Heidegger claims that human beings always press into some or the other possibilities and because of this pressing objects meaningfully appear to us. We cannot encounter an object as a mere object; it always has to have a meaningful presence to us.[37] Thus, our understanding of other things is always a hermeneutical understanding. In the following, I would briefly discuss and will highlight some of the features of the concept of the phenomenological world in the light of Heidegger's concept of the world to demonstrate how far the phenomenological world and *saṃsāra* commensurate with each other.

Heidegger's phenomenology argues that *Dasein* or the human existence is always-already *"being-in-the-world"* or always exists spacio-temporally.[38] The "being" in the being-in-the-world is the meaningfulness of things. It elucidates the fact that "the meaning giving context opened up by and as ex-sistence"[39] or in other words, the human existence precedes this meaningfulness. The phrase being-in-the-world actually refers to the always-already existing meaningful engagements of human beings with the world of intelligibility. Briefly, the concept of world in phenomenology describes one's phenomenological experience of other living and non-living entities due to her intentionality. The subjective experiential reality of the outer-physical world creates the phenomenological world. The world in the phrase phenomenological world does not denote the entire worldly space; rather, it points to the world of an individual. Each individual dwells in this "open space" that allows one to take things "as this-or-that and thus to understand their "being"—that is, how and like what they are currently meaningful."[40] The concept of the phenomenological world discards the ultimate universal objective truth of the world, instead, it demonstrates that through one's engagements, an individual establishes her relation to other beings and creates the "phenomenological world." Heidegger says that in the human ex-sistence, things just cannot stand separately, or it cannot stand alone. According to Heidegger, "world" is not a realm constituted by objects rather each individual encounter meaningful intelligibility of objects in everyday existence as she presses into some possibility or other, and that intelligibility of things generated through those pressing into possibilities or intention to accomplish certain roles that constitutes one's world.[41] The possibilities one is pressing into, decide how each of our worlds would be like. In this way, each of our worlds is entirely personalized.[42] Due to the difference in meaningful presence of things, each of our world is different from the other's world. In other words, my world appears to me because of my purpose and pressing into different possibilities. In this sense, the phenomenological world is capable of capturing the sense of relational reality, one of the main attributes of *saṃsāra*, quite precisely. Moreover, the other attribute, the notion of dynamicity can also be grasped if we understand the connection between the phenomenological world, possibilities, and the external world. As discussed, the creation of the phenomenological world is contingent on pressing into possibilities, and solely, in the light of the possibilities things become meaningful. Therefore, any changes in possibilities can actually lead to changes in the meaningful presence of entities as well as can alter one's phenomenological world. Thus, the concept of phenomenological world can very well accommodate the dynamicity of one's surroundings as outer changes modify possibilities and in turn, alter or curb one's relation to other beings and entities of the outer physical world. This justifies that the aforementioned malleability of the phenomenological world, in turn, makes an individual receptive towards any changes occurring in the external world. In this manner, the notion of the phenomenological world is also capable of capturing the dynamicity one's surroundings.

Although the notion of phenomenological world can capture an individual's relational reality with and the dynamic presence of her surroundings, akin to *saṃsāra*, these two terms cannot directly complement each other in terms of capturing the exact meaning. In other words, the phenomenological world is only capable of expressing the meaning-bearing-capacity of the concept *saṃsāra*. Therefore, there is a possibility that further active engagements with these two terms might lead to the retranslation of both of these in their respective languages. Sarukkai's proposal to explore translation as a method, could open up further avenues to inquire how retranslation can add new possible meanings to these concepts in their respective traditions.[43] No doubt this engagement will start with ambiguity, nevertheless, it will definitely extend the semantic space of *saṃsāra* as well as the phenomenological world, and in this particular case, it will also extend the notion of environment. Therefore, the unique relationship of human beings with their surroundings that have been captured in the islanders' narratives could fundamentally transform our understanding about the environment.

SIGNIFICANCE OF SAṂSĀRA AND PHENOMENOLOGICAL WORLD

From the field narratives, I realize that there is hardly any uniform conception of environment that exists in the context of the human—

environment relationship. To capture, the dynamicity and the relational reality explained by the islanders, in this essay, I attempt to find a new term to represent the same. Simultaneously, this essay also provides an account of how translating a term like environment can get complicated if one tries to capture the experiential notion of it. I show why there is a necessity to ascribe new terms to capture the existing relationship that the islanders possess with their surroundings. At this moment, I should acknowledge that I limit myself from conducting an in-depth exploration of the influence of these two concepts on each other, especially, in terms of exploring its linguistic contribution. However, these different comprehensions can definitely provide a fresh outlook to rethink the conventional articulation of the human—environment relationship.

To conclude, I would like to elaborate on to what extent *saṃsāra* and its translation as the phenomenological world, can contribute to the emerging discourse of ecophenomenology. Before elaborating on that I would also like to highlight that if one accepts the notion of *saṃsāra* to articulate human beings' relationship with their surroundings, then how the approach to save or protect the Sundarbans can get radically altered.

In the context of the Sundarbans, the conventional environmental protection and conservation measures function with the universally defined principles to mitigate environmental changes and consequently, promote a static idea of the environment. The Sundarbans, being demarcated as a biodiversity hotspot of India, a tiger reserve, and a heritage site always remains in the purview of ecologists and conservationists. Numerous national and international reports are making the prediction that the vulnerability of this cluster of islands to climate change, is going to rise in the coming years. These predictions are strengthening the discourse that these islands need to be protected through the rigorous implementation of various conservation and development projects. For the same, in the recent past, the Sundarbans has witnessed a plethora of projects directed toward conserving and preserving its land and ecosystem, particularly from sea water invasion. This kind of initiatives, for the sake of preserving the ecosystems, is prone to separate the inhabitant of this area by limiting their access to forests and the sea.[44] In another article, I have demonstrated that this kind of attempt is an outcome of an "Abrahamic conception"[45] of the Sundarbans's land. No doubt, these types of projects for protecting the Sundarbans often create tensions between the insiders or the inhabitants, and the outsiders. This essay illuminates that instead of the conventional way of saving the Sundarbans region by focusing on the static notion of environment or basing on a conceptual understanding derived primarily from ecology, it is far more important to protect the essence of the Sundarbans, as unveiled through the phenomenological experience of the islanders. Considering I have shown that in these islands, the concept of static environment is itself an alien one, preserving and conserving the same notion of environment also seems outlandish for the islanders. Therefore, I posit, there is an urgent need to bring an ethic that can uphold this dynamicity and relational reality of the environment or can endorse this notion of *saṃsāra* to preserve the Sundarbans, in its true form. The articulation of the phenomenological experience of the Sundarbans as *saṃsāra* portrays a unique understanding of the region and reaffirm the need to focus on the place and its inhabitants to protect and conserve the essence of the place. Furthermore, I see, it is important to highlight the bearings of phenomenological experience of *saṃsāra*, on the discourse of ecophenomenology. This plausibly would tease out the larger implications of the notion of *saṃsāra*, instead of just being a regional concept.

As already mentioned, I see *saṃsāra* though being a regional concept, has the potential to make some unique contributions to the emerging stream of ecophenomenology. To overcome the prevailing technological domination, the literature of ecophenomenology primarily advocates for poetic dwelling. Toadvine underlines that poetic dwelling is one of the key concepts of ecophenomenology.[46] According to Toadvine, poetic dwelling is only possible when our engagements with things are phenomenological, instead of being a metaphysically predefined one. In this context, the notion of *saṃsāra*, as we can see now, does not presume any predefined notion of environment, indeed, it can be taken as an example of true acknowledgement of prereflective experience of one's surroundings. *Saṃsāra* thereby portrays an authentic mode of dwelling where an individual becomes receptive towards the dynamicity of the outside world and also rightfully accepts the changing feature of life or inner world as well as the outer world. Moreover, it exemplifies an authentic mode of dwelling as it represents entirely a personalized world where the meaningful presence of things, the relationship one pursues with these, and their significance is entirely one's own. In this mode of dwelling, one neither gets restricted into any theoretical understanding, nor devalues the presence of things in its true forms. Hence, *saṃsāra* eventually demonstrates what poetic dwelling could mean in today's world. It portrays how a place become a "deeply humanized world"[47] for the inhabitants and how that, subsequently, turns a place into a homeplace. As being indicative of poetic dwelling, the notion of *saṃsāra* and the phenomenological world could be embraced to preserve the essence of a place that does not conform to any pervasive conceptions, rather, remains liminal in its very nature. Preserving the essence in this manner, I see, delineates an avenue to uphold the integrity of the fourfold and thus, offers a scope to shape our relationship with our surroundings in the mode of poetic dwelling, beyond the prevailing technological mode of revelation.

Saṃsāra is far from being a mere illustration of poetic dwelling, it further enriches the concept of poetic dwelling by adding two significant features. First, the concept of poetic dwelling as it gets incorporated into the literature of ecophenomenology, usually highlights the need for human beings to reveal the interconnectedness of nature and subsequently, to realize their place in that interconnected milieu to possibly reach a more harmonious state of the human—environment relationship. The concept of *saṃsāra*, however, accentuates neither on the environment nor on human beings, but rather on the relationship, and more importantly, it attempts to illuminate how that relationship gets fundamentally shaped by the intentionality of human beings— the pivotal characteristic of the human existence. As I see it, poetic dwelling as a concept has not yet explored the role of the creation of a meaningful object realm due to one's intentionality and a proper inclusion of the notion of *saṃsāra* would definitely enrich the concept in demarcating ways to incorporate the relational realities of individuals as well as understanding the bearings of those realities on the human—environment relationship.

Second, as being an example of poetic dwelling, *saṃsāra* can introduce the notion of change in the conceptualization of poetic dwelling. The notion of *saṃsāra* precisely demonstrates that changes in the physical world always guide our relationship with it. Or in other words, changes in the outside, open up new possibilities and provide opportunities for an individual to press into those different ones. As a result, changes in the outside world clearly induce changes in one's phenomenological world. Owing to that, in the realm of *saṃsāra* instead of curbing or impeding, an individual becomes fully in tune with the changes that are relentlessly occurring in the surroundings and thus, attains an authentic relationship with the surroundings. This deep sense of acceptance could invoke a completely new dimension to the conceptualization of poetic dwelling. Moreover, this notion of dynamicity, as being a permanent but rather an unexplored dimension of the human—environment relationship, could be a novel contribution to ecophenomenology. Any future scholarly works and explorations based on this articulation of *saṃsāra*, would definitely ensure that a due importance gets vested in the notion of dynamicity or the notion of change.

KALPITA BHAR PAUL is a scholar at Manipal Centre for Philosophy and Humanities, Manipal University, India. Her PhD dissertation explores the phenomenological understanding of the human—environment relationship and its implications for environmental ethics. She is particularly interested in Heidegger's phenomenology and its bearings on environmental philosophy.

NOTES

The author thanks Manipal Centre for Philosophy and Humanities, Manipal University for providing them with the support for this research. The author also extends her gratitude to her PhD supervisor, Prof. Meera Baindur. The field work for this study would not have been possible without the generous sharing by the Development Research Communication and Services Centre, Kolkata and the Indraprastha Srijan Welfare Society, Pathorpratima, West Bengal, who provided the assistance of their field infrastructures, networks, and field staffs. The author also acknowledges those people of the Sundarbans who gave their time and shared their life stories for this research as well as two referees for and the editor of *Environment, Space, Place* who helped me formulate this paper better.

1. Charismatic species are large animal species with widespread popular appeal, like Tiger, Elephant, Lion, etc.
2. Development and Planning Department, Government of West Bengal. *District Human Development Report: South 24 Parganas.* HDRCC, (UNDP, October 2009), 291.

Accessed http://www.undp.org/content/dam/india/docs/hdr_south24_parganas_2009_full_report.pdf.

3. For more details about this methodology and its relevance in environmental humanities see Meera Baindur and Kalpita Bhar Paul, "Mapping the observer in the observation in Anthropocene: A Methodological Exploration." *Humanities Circle* 3, no. 2 (2015): 61–81.

4. FLDN stands for Field narrative. Henceforth, FLDN will indicate excerpts from the field narratives.

5. FLDN.

6. FLDN.

7. FLDN.

8. FLDN.

9. FLDN.

10. Yi-fu-Tuan, "Place: An Experiential Perspective," *Geographical Review* 65 (1975): 151–65.

11. Yi-fu-Tuan, "Language and the Making of Place: A Narrative-Descriptive Approach," *Annals of the Association of American Geographers* 81 (1991): 686.

12. Ibid., 686.

13. As the purpose of this essay is to find an appropriate term to describe the islanders' experience of their environment, I am consciously refraining from using the term environment and using "surroundings" instead, especially, when I am referring to the islanders' perception.

14. As the mother-tongue of the narrators is Bengali, a regional language of India, I attempt to see whether the equivalent terms of various chosen English words in Bengali, can precisely grasp their notion.

15. Source: (http://www.etymonline.com/index.php?term=environment).

16. Source: (http://www.etymonline.com/index.php?term=environment).

17. P. Marshall, *Nature's Web: Rethinking our Place on Earth* (1st ed,) (London: Simon and Schuster Ltd., 1992).

18. See Kate Soper, *What is Nature?* (USA, Blackwell, 1995); Meera Baindur, *Nature in Indian Philosophy and Cultural Traditions* (India: Springer, 2015) for an elaborate account of the term "nature."

19. The word *saṃsāra* is actually a Sanskrit word. In Bengali, *saṃsāra* is pronounced as *sangsar*. In the rest of this essay, however, I will use *saṃsāra* to denote both its meanings in Sanskrit and in Bengali.

20. W. S. K. Cameron. "Must Environmental Philosophy Relinquish the Concept of Nature? A Hermeneutic Reply to Steven Vogel," in *Interpreting Nature: The Emerging Field of Environmental Hermeneutics,* ed. Forrest Clingerman et al. (New York: Fordham University Press, 2014), 102–20.

21. Hans-Georg Gadamer, *Truth and Method* , (2nd Rev. ed.), trans. W. Glean-Deopel, ed. J. Cumming and G. Barden, rev. Joel Weinsheimer and Donald G. Marshal (New York: Crossroads Pres, 1991).

22. Cameron. "Must Environmental Philosophy Relinquish the Concept of Nature?," 112.

23. Michael P. Ryan, "Samasa and Saṃsāra: Suffering, Death and rebirth in 'The metamorphosis,'" *The German Quarterly* 72 (1999): 133.

24. David Loy. "The difference between Samsāra and 'Nirvāṇa,'" *Philosophy of East and West* 33 (1983): 355.

25. Ryan, "Samasa and Saṃsāra," 133–52.

26. Loy, "The difference between Samsāra and "Nirvāṇa."

27. Matilal, "Duhkha, Nirvana and Holy Men," in *The Collected Essay of Bimal Krishna Matilal: Philosophy, Culture and Religion: Ethics and Epics,"* ed. Jonardan Ganeri (New Delhi: Oxford University Press, 2002), 369–81.

28. Ibid., 373.

29. Ibid., 371.

30. Danto 1972, 48, as cited in Matilal "Duhkha, Nirvana and Holy Men," 374.

31. Cameron, "Must Environmental Philosophy Relinquish the Concept of Nature?"

32. Sundar Sarukkai, "Translation as Method: Implications for history of science," in *The Circulating Knowledge Between Britain, India and China*, ed. B. Lightman, L. Stewart, & G. McOuat. (Leiden: Bill Press, 2013), 311–29.

33. Ibid., 314.

34. Ibid., 326.

35. H. L. Dreyfus, *Being-in-the-World: A commentary on Heidegger's Being and Time, Division I.* (Cambridge: MIT Press, 1991), 7.

36. G. M. Reiners, "Understanding the Differences between Husserl's (Descriptive) and Heidegger's (Interpretive) Phenomenological Research," *Journal of Nursing & Care* 1 (2012): 119, doi: 10.4172/2167–1168.1000119.

37. Thomas Sheehan, *Making Sense of Heidegger: A Paradigm Shift.* (London and New York: Rowman and Littlefield, 2015), 112.

38. L Finlay, "Debating Phenomenological Research Method," *Phenomenology and Practice* 3 (2009): 11.

39. Sheehan, *Making Sense of Heidegger*, 11.

40. Ibid., 70.

41. Martin E. Heidegger, *Being and Time*, trans. Joan Stambaugh. (Albany: State University of New York, 1953), 52–3 and 97–107.

42. Ibid., 135–44.

43. Sarukkai, "Translation as Method," 328.

44. P. Ghosh, 2014. "Subsistence and Biodiversity Conservation in the Sundarban Biosphere Reserve, West Bengal, India." Theses and Dissertations—Geography. Paper 26. http://uknowledge.uky.edu/geography_etds/26, 78–158.

45. For more details see Kalpita Bhar Paul and Meera Baindur "Leopold's Land Ethic in the Sundarbans: A Phenomenological Approach" forthcoming in *Environmental Ethics* 38, no. 3. Here, I have borrowed the notion of Abrahamic Conception from Leopold's Land Ethics.

46. Ted Toadvine. "Phenomenology and Environmental Ethics," in *Oxford Handbook of Environmental Ethics*, ed. S. M. Gardiner and A. Thompson. (Oxford: Oxford University Press, 2015), Ch 14.

47. Tuan, "Language and the Making of Place," 686.

Borders

*Landscapes in Catalan Fiction Today: Feeling of Restlessness
Produced by the Border in the Work of Vicenç Pagès, Joan Todó,
and Francesc Serés*

MARIA PUIG PARNAU

Abstract

This article will analyze the feeling of restlessness that we discover in the representation of the border areas, seen as extreme and paradigmatic landscapes of contemporary society. The analysis is based on three narrative works of current Catalan literature: Dies de frontera *(Frontier days; 2014) by Vicenç Pagèsa;* La pell de la frontera *(The skin of the frontier; 2014) by Francesc Serés, and* L'horitzó primer *(The first horizon; 2014) by Joan Todó. Traditional Catalan— and European—literature, has long since lent great weight to literary representation of landscape in the creation of identity and culture. Now, however, with the desolate, degraded and forgotten landscapes of the peripheries and borders, the narrative of place speaks to us of personal and collective crises. In recent decades, academics speak of a* spatial turn *in the humanities, and some even talk of a shift in civilization tied to the landscape. Catalan fiction is a good example of this shift. We shall analyze these three books to see how this place is perceived aesthetically and define the feeling of disquiet and restlessness which emerges, in the end, from these specific and deeply human observations.*

INTRODUCTION

We live in a world in which it seems impossible to look upon landscape as we used to. In the not-too-distant past, the land was regarded as separate and defined entities (town and country, areas of agriculture and forestry, the village and outskirts); now, modern-day landscapes are defined by hybridization, fragmentation and imprecision. Urban sprawl is the result of the rapid expansion in tertiary industries and tourism; the technological revolution; the boom in real estate and even the effects of a certain crisis in public space.[1] And it is not only the appearance of places that has changed, but also the relationship of people with these places. Contemporary society is marked by movement, speed, change and globalization. The pressure on natural resources means that the ecological crisis is now one of the issues that defines the twenty-first century. And we continually see how each area "adopts" diverse waves of identities, and likewise, how each identity can adopt several territories, or perhaps cannot adopt any at all. It seems, therefore, that it no longer makes sense to recreate the purity of landscapes and that a certain amount of tact is now required when associating a landscape—as was the case throughout the nineteenth and for most of the twentieth century—with a narrative of identity in which the individual and society are rooted. Now, surrounded by all the latest modern conveniences, the individual realizes that he is losing the landscape; that his sense of place is changing, that *place* is melting away.

How do we see landscape now? The ethical and aesthetic implications of this degradation of the landscape are deep and clearly visible. Romantic sensibilities were firmly based upon pure landscapes of natural beauty through which man experienced a transcendent communion. But our landscapes become less pure day by day. The nationalism of the nineteenth century created stories of identity based on territory because, for a long time, having power meant having land. But now power is virtual, intangible and global. So how do we see landscape now? And how do we understand and reconstruct the imaginary that we had built up?

At present, western art and thought is looking again at landscape and is doing so with a reflective and critical attitude. Some authors even speak of a shift in civilization; a renewed interest towards landscape as an artistic theme and as an object of reflection that demonstrates the need to, once again, bring people closer not only to their environment and to nature, but also to the sensory experience of the world, of things and of their very existence.[2]

LANDSCAPE IN CONTEMPORARY CATALAN LITERATURE

In the context of this social and aesthetic interest in landscape, we can include the very latest Catalan fiction, which is the basis of this article. The landscape has long been a key element in the literary and cultural history of Catalonia; one needs go no further than *Oda a la pàtria* (Ode to the fatherland) or *Canigó*,[3] texts which are heavily charged with landscape and which are widely considered as foundational pieces of Catalan culture. Then there is *Solitud* (Solitude) or the works Joaquim Ruyra and the books of Josep Pla.[4] All of these are major names in Catalan literature and all train their sights again and again on the landscape in order to speak of it, praise it and explore it and build an identity or express a feeling. Despite distinguished exceptions such as *Camí de sirga* (The towpath),[5] Catalan fiction subsequently tended to focus on urban areas and even undefined or empty spaces, of which Quim Monzo's work is the best example. In other words, there was a long tradition in which the landscape was mythologized, followed by two decades, the eighties and nineties, in which this landscape was forgotten. But then, in Catalan literature, as in other European literatures, the first decades of our century saw a revitalised and renewed spatial sensitivity.[6] How do our storytellers see the landscape now? What do they see there?

Within the Catalan literary scene, there are a number of young writers who, in recent years, have published works that stand out for their observation and exploration of landscape, for their choice of present-day landscapes and for shifting their attention to the peripheries and rural areas of Catalonia today. Furthermore, they look upon this landscape from up close, but critically, raw and stripped of myths, creating profound tales about the sense of place and contemporary human identity. Examples of this trend include works by Edgar Illas, Vicenç Pagès, Adrià Pujol, Marta Rojals, Toni Sala, Francesc Serés and Joan Todó.[7] Many others could still be added to this list. They are not works of regionalism or bucolic escapism. The discourse of these works begins in some small location and ends up speaking of a broader and more profound reality: the loss of landscape, the loss of place and everything that place represents for the individual and the community (memory, home, language, stability, references, harmony) and a consequent feeling of bewilderment, pain or anguish. They are bold texts, never wallowing in nostalgia, that connect loss with thought, tradition with modernity, place with universality. They also blend various literary styles of fiction with those of nonfiction, such as biography, documentary or essay.

The representation of Catalan contemporary narrative landscape allows us to analyse this lived-in landscape in the present, based on the experience of the *I*. These writers have chosen the native landscape of their characters and the narration begins from the moment they return to it and stay there. Furthermore, in the real world, we discover that these landscapes are also the places where the authors themselves grew up. This context alerts us, on the one hand, to the frontier style of the narratives, which move between fiction and reality, with some texts that can be considered as literary autobiographies or poetical documentaries. On the other hand, this also alerts us to the importance of the *I*, the instrument which forms the story of place, with their everyday experience.

It is impossible not to link this idea of "story of landscape" with Michel de Certeau's thesis. In *The Practice of Everyday Life*, the French sociologist talks about the construction of a story of space through the everyday experience of people in that space. According to him, it is such stories formed by everyday life that transform a place, which is an entity of outward, univocal and stable positions, into a space which is animate, mobile and lived.[8] This article does not use the terminology in the sense that de Certeau uses it, but rather, favours the distinction made by Joan Nogué and Marc Augé, closer in time and discipline to this article. In his essay *Paisatge, territori i societat civil* (Landscape, territory and civil society), Nogué talks about "space" in terms of abstraction, whereas he talks of "place" in terms of anthropology, identity and emotion.[9] Similarly, Augé contrasts non-places to an anthropological place that is identitary, relational and historic.[10] It is a concrete and symbolic construction that gives sense to its culture for those who live there and intelligibility to those who observes it.[11] This is the sense of "place" used in this article. While the word "space"—currently widely appropriated in the service and IT industries—is reserved for the abstract constructions not formed by the personal relationships that come from experience.

That said, the notion of "story" on Michel de Certeau's work is indispensable. It is the story which, based on everyday experience, give sense and life to the abstract space. The construction of this type of story is what we witness in these texts. De Certeau assimilates "story" to the spoken language, as if the space were an imposed written language which is consumed as a reading and create and recreate as a speaking or a story. Therefore, the story is alive, changing and relational. Always from the point of view of the *I*, in close and human contact with the otherness on the landscape and landscape itself. Always through everyday life, the story guides us, transports us, it is our *metaphorai*, it organizes and also creates our landscape.[12]

THE BORDER IN CONTEMPORARY CATALAN FICTION

In contemporary Catalan narrative, we find new ways to represent the landscape. But, not only has the way these authors talk about landscape changed but, in many cases, we also find new landscapes, new landscapes in our Catalan culture and, among these, the border has a distinguished place. The stories are set in places that we could call *non-central*. The one closest to the Catalan capital, Barcelona, is set in the periphery of the city and in the county of El Maresme, further up the coast; and the author who examines the mythologized lands of Empordà resolves to make them raw and intimate through his narrative style. But amongst all of these backwater areas, we find the one most isolated of all: the border. Three of these books focus on the landscapes of border: *Dies de frontera* (Border days), by Vicenç Pagès; *La pell de la frontera* (The skin of the border), by Francesc Serés and *L'horitzó primer* (The first horizon), by Joan Todó.[13] We will now explore the type of border organized and created by the story.

It cannot be said that Catalan literature has ignored this landscape. It has been dealt with on other occasions. The border appears in the wonderful work of Marià Vayreda, *La punyalada* (The stab; 1904), in *Terres de l'Ebre* (1932) by Sebastian J. Arbó and perhaps *Camí de sirga* could also be considered to be a story of the border, along with the many texts produced by republicans describing their flight into exile after the Spanish civil war. But what is certain is that the border is a very important element in the current narrative of landscape and that its metaphorical and stylistic value is new. And this is what I want to look at through the three books in question here. The border is a creative engine of content and form. Suffice to look at the titles which, literally or metaphorically, point out the line, the limit, where we find ourselves.

Before continuing, I will briefly summarise the plots of these books to give us some context. *Dies de frontera*, which earned Vicenç Pagès the Sant Jordi Prize in 2013, is set in Figueres, near the border between

Catalonia—or Spain—and France. It tells the story of love and separation of Teresa and Paul, a couple approaching their forties who, after
many years of a stable relationship, are going through a 'problematic'
time. We witness the crisis of the couple and, in effect, the existential crisis of the two characters. Paul endures this crisis as he wanders
around the streets of Figueres while, Teresa, who takes on a more central role in the story, experiences it at the border itself. One day, returning by train from Girona, Teresa meets a man and ends up going with
him for a weekend at the border. And the reader, with an adroit external
narrative voice as our guide, goes along with them. We stroll through
the village of Els Limits and the town of La Jonquera, in a journey of
peculiar proximity. There, the protagonist spends a few days with the
man and, above all, walks, observes and takes stock.

While this novel takes place near the great state border in northern
Catalonia, the other two are located in regional borders. In terms of
government, these may be less strictly controlled, but for the people
who live there, they are perceived and experienced as borders all the
same. L'horitzó primer, by Joan Todó, is set in La Sénia, a village right
next to the boundary line between Catalonia and Valencia, while Fran-
cisco Serés, in La pell de la frontera, focuses on Lleida and La Franja
(The strip), an area of Catalan-speaking territories in Aragon border-
ing Catalonia. These are undoubtedly borders; fine lines on the map,
but lines that demarcate important linguistic and cultural changes on a
scale of profound proximity—the only valid scale in these stories.

L'horitzó primer tells the story of a young man's return to his village,
La Sénia. The protagonist goes there because he has been asked to give
the opening speech of the local festival, a task which is entrusted to
villagers who have left La Sénia and triumphed in the wider world. But
he, despite having published several books and having lived in Barcelona for many years, does not see himself as a great success or as having
left at all. He is approaching forty, cannot find work and has decided
to stay at his parents' home, in the village. There, he will observe the
village and write. The result is the text we read, a text that combines
the past and present in the same world, in which the narrator is split
into the I, a voice into the character, who speaks to the bewildered you,
the character with presence in the narration, and who probes his per-

sonal crisis while also investigating a place in crisis, a quiet village full of memories, still welcoming, but also degraded, empty and tedious.

La pell de la frontera is a narrative work which, despite the literary nature of the texts, consists of reports written in a documentary prose which is lyrical but realistic, biographical and experiential. Francesc Serés, who appears by name in some of the texts, brings together fourteen stories in this volume, dated between 2003 and 2011, about his visits and his understanding of the Catalan-Aragon border. He deals with themes such as immigration, the modernization of the countryside and the land, the globalization of the economy and trade and social polarization. What unifies the texts is the experience of the border. That is, to find out, to *know* that you are between two worlds, two landscapes in contact that rub against each other, that scratch at each other but also embrace, as Serés puts it; two worlds that meet and touch with everything they are. And, in this way, the border becomes a mirror, the harshest but at the same time the clearest mirror of all, of the world, of the other and of the *I* that thinks about it all.

BORDERS

In these three books, then, the border is, first of all, the setting, but it becomes evident that it has other meanings as well, and that they influence the content and style of each work.

These works contain stylistic borders. That is to say, the fact of constructing a text in a border setting does not leave the text unaffected. The works differ from each other, but all three are fragmentary, because contemporary landscape, as I said at the start, is fragmented and it is at the border, more than anywhere else, where the cracks are seen. This is reflected in the structure of these texts. Serés, created *La pell de la frontera* from fourteen stories with beginnings and endings, separated by considerable margins in space and time, each of which can be read alone, unconnected to any of the others. Each tells a different story, a different experience, of the border. We hear the story of a very young boy, Hakeem and a lonely old man, Juli, who takes Hakeem and his family into his home until, one day, they go away and leave him lonelier still. We hear an agricultural engineer describing the fields with heavy irony and a corrosive criticism of current farming practices. We see pictures, both desolate and beautiful: the makeshift huts of immigrants among the orchards and the shiny skin of youngsters bathing in a dirty river. Vicenç Pagès, meanwhile, as he had done in other books, bases his novel on countless quick-fire chapters which, like a mosaic, form something whole, but which are, in essence, small parts, brief flashes of the lives of the characters and of the thoughts of the narrative voice. No longer than three pages in most cases, some speak of the central character's childhood, others reproduce fragments of his thesis, others describe scenes set in the present, or make historical notes, copy Facebook profiles or list the likes and dislikes of the characters. In both books, the texts become a unitary whole thanks to the common thread of the border and to the narrative voice that gives expression to it. Joan Todó's novel, meanwhile, is more unified in structure, but is based on the dual role of the narrator, who is always divided into an *I* and a *You* who never really work out how to get along, and who see their internal borders explicitly. In addition, time is also split into two, as Todó, explaining this landscape as a place made from time, conjures up stories from the past in the village but also characters, people from other times who, much like ghosts, slip into the narrative, let themselves be seen; they appear and disappear; they speak.

The border of these texts is also a border between genres. As noted previously, each author writes about a lived-in landscape: the landscape of the author's biography and the fictional landscape are the same. They are works of literature, art, creation, but the link with reality is very marked, so, in some cases, this link and their approach to describing these places mean that the books switch between fiction and non-fiction. Of the three, the clearest example of this is Serés. *La pell de la frontera* is literary reportage with a heavy autobiographical and essayist bent. It is, indeed, on the border between these genres. And yet the same happens, on specific and different levels, in the other books. The narrator of *L'horitzó primer* is a literary type who has remarkable similarities with the one who created him: Joan Todó is also from La Sénia; he also returned there after finding himself without work in Barcelona; he also is a writer. Here too, the borders are thin and limits unclear. Furthermore, the writing styles are also combined in these works: as explained before, Pagès mixes fictional narrative with excerpts of historical accounts, with brief essay notes, lists and texts taken from social networks. We might easily ask ourselves whether or not we are reading a novel, but we already know, in the contemporary world, that boundaries are made of fine lines. Serés, for his part, in his volume of short stories, includes one which is in fact a collection of photographs taken by the author himself: a "little handbook of ephemeral architecture" which depicts the "facilities", i.e., the makeshift dwellings of the immigrants in the fruit plantations in La Franja. The border has led the writer to make these narrative decisions and the reader arrives at the border thanks to the literary form. Because the border is a fine line, and we cannot easily distinguish between content and form. Clearly, the form of each of these works also creates meaning.

If we return to what is considered, strictly speaking, to be content, and bearing in mind the brief synopses given above, we can see that, in addition to being a location on a map and a place that stirs genres and narrative approaches, the border is also a decidedly intimate, interior and personal border. Each of the individuals we listen to in these stories carries the border within themselves, because they see it and live it. In an essay on the motel and contemporary lifestyles of American and Western societies called *Common Place. The American Motel*, Bruce Bégout defines the motel as a mental space because people and stories settled on it are and become people or stories on the margin, as schematized and simplified as the space form, as the motel. In the stories we are dealing with here, the border is exactly that: a mental space where the place mobilizes the perceptions, the intentions and the feelings of the characters. Place and thought take shape together; they mix. From this point on, the various components of this personal experience of the border become confused and become connected, because place is, as Henri Lefebvre says, mental, physical and social at the same time, like a three-way dialectical unity. It is difficult to analyse a place without talking about these components as aspects of one and the same entity, and it is distorting to understand the landscape as only one of these aspects.[14] Besides, if we are analysing literary places, I have no hesitation in saying that place, in addition, is formalistic.

The main characters in two of these books are crossing borders, going through moments of crisis in their personal lives, while Serés' narrator manages, in part, to keep any such crisis at arm's length. They are reassessing everything, or almost everything, after a situation that makes them question what they thought was stable (losing their job and not finding another, approaching forty and having to return to the parental home, losing the partner who had seemed to be theirs for life). It forces them into a period of introspection, an intimate reflection that comes with a certain dissatisfaction or personal restlessness. What is more, this feeling emerges at the border. It is at the border, looking at this place, where they get to know—and we get to know—the *I*, where they experience their own border. The individuals who move on the margins are people in transit, as Pagès says in various chapter titles, or 'in process' as Bégout says, "beings *on the brink of*, but who have not yet achieved their goal, nor decided upon they want."[15] The place and the restlessness, the exterior and the thoughts, go together. This internal crisis is expressed because they are at the border and they are at the border because they are in crisis. The statement can be made in both senses. Both of these things, *place* and *I*, go together. They are on the edge, since they live in landscapes on the edge, and if the landscape is degraded and on the edge, then human feeling has much the same nature.

This link between the expression of the self and the expression of the landscape, both lost and lost to each other, is the basis of the experience of the contemporary landscape. Is this everyday experience what forms the story of place. Take, for example, this fragment which Todó's narrator gives at the end of the book:

In fact, much of the horizon you see from the window belongs to the municipality of Rossell. And on Facebook, the place, if you try to say you live here, is "La Cenia, Comunidad Valenciana", "La Sénia, Oran, Algèria", or "Sénia, Koulikoro, Mali". . . . You click "Like" to indicate that you are there, as if you're afraid that no one remembers you. Oran, Koulikoro, Mali. If whatever is not on the internet nowadays does not exist, maybe this village doesn't exist, perhaps it is a fiction. You put out your cigarette. . . . Behind the computer, neatly arranged, you have the three fat volumes of the last course you did. You refresh. Nothing. Refresh. Nothing. You open the mail again from the guy at the magazine, inspecting it carefully. Back to your inbox. Nothing. Refresh. Nothing. Refresh. Nothing.[16]

Even Serés reports a human crisis in *La pell de la frontera*. Even though it is unclear whether he is going through his own personal crisis, since his role is of more of a reporter, even he, due to this experience of the border and because of his close-up exploration, describes a deep and intimate crisis. He says, for example:

> One of the farmers from Torres de Segre who I spoke to last week told me that these people had come so that we should not we lose sight of the world. He said it was a warning about where the world was going. Not where it was heading, but where it was going. . . . We still think there is a safety net that can withstand everything, that life here is secure, stable, and we will never have need of a boat to cross some strange sea. There aren't any such nets.[17]

> Here there aren't any membranes; here there is the excessive heat, the smell of grass and the wet soil of the vegetable patch, the rusty tin cans and excrement, the shacks of plastic, pallet and corrugated iron, the abrasive heat. . . . The real *Celebration of Diversity* festival should take place here on the outskirts of Alcarràs. It's as if what they attempted to set up here were a part of the reality that we cannot touch. . . . For me, there is no distance, I carry these remains within me and I hope they never disappear.[18]

We are reminded of our fragility and that of the world we live in. Although we might have thought we lived within limits of security, stability and welfare, the degradation and poverty are ours also. Looking at these desolate landscapes, degraded and barren, is to look at who we are as individuals and as a community. Citing Bégout, "the environment has ceased to offer any guidance, to dispel my misgivings."[19] In Serés' story, reality eventually surpasses the limits and borders; he marks out other borders. Saidí (his hometown in La Franja) is not Europe, he says. The immigrants cannot set up camp like this in the Plaça de Catalunya in Barcelona, or in the centre of some big city. But it makes sense to do it here, in the small farming towns of Lleida and La Franja. This is what borders are, too—ones that separate the centres from the periphery, the space of the world from the place, what is global from what is local, large scale from closeness, systems from people. And at the same time, says Serés, no matter how many lines are drawn up, it all ends up being mishmash and tension; "the world arrives everywhere," he keeps saying, and there are borders that are always there, that come back and that go much further than we thought. The world comes home. We all live in the midst of the border. We just need to want to see it and remember it, he says.

This vision of the border by Serés leads us to another aspect of the border experience: the intimate and personal crisis is inextricably linked to the social crisis. Serés feels this social problem to be a human, interior fact and one which affects him as an inhabitant of this place and as a person. The protagonist of *L'horitzó primer* also expresses his personal crisis within the framework of a social crisis. He has no job, largely because of the period of economic crisis in which he lives and of his country's low regard for professions involving the humanities and letters. Furthermore, upon his return to the village, he becomes aware that some of the furniture stores used to employ so many people have now closed, and many live their lives as best they can. And he also notices the feeling of abandonment among the people of La Sénia who, faced also with a crisis of a political nature, joke about being stuck in a no man's land between a Valencia which might be more Spanish and a Catalonia which could be more Catalan:

> As for us, they (the Catalans) put us in Spain. ¿Can't you hear them? Other side of the River Ebro this, other side of the Ebro that, it's all the other side of the Ebro. They don't think of us here as Catalans.[20]

Even the protagonist of *Dies de frontera*, who seems immersed only in problems of love, observes the border, at La Jonquera and sees signs of social crisis. People shop and people go, but no one looks and no one thinks. This woman, who goes on this little local journey and who therefore looks at it differently, sees it all as unnatural and uncomfortable and superficial: the roundabout, the brothels, the supermarkets full of alcohol and tobacco, the shopping malls and car parks. Huge, unique, they consume us. Surrounding it all, the Pyrenees go almost unseen and if the forests do get noticed, what stands out are the charred remains of the fire, also huge, which burned there in the summer of 2012.[21] In the midst of this inhospitable site, the protagonist, profoundly bewildered, cannot stop herself exclaiming "But what *is* this?"[22] And what is more, they are on the border with France, the border of the Republican exile, and in the midst of all this hurriedness, the narrator and his characters focus for a moment on a plaque in Portbou in memory of Walter Benjamin and remember the poet, Machado, and think of all the anonymous exiles who passed through these same places. Memory, and the loss of memory linked to the degradation of the landscape, is a common element in all three books. Todó makes an immense effort to fit into his account all the possible history of the place and the Civil War references and the misery of Francoism emerges unexpectedly in Serés' work in order to show us that we do forget and, perhaps, to make us remember. Memory is collective and personal, but always present and near, in this observation of the landscape.

With the thematic content of these three books, the authors are reflecting on political concepts that are very much alive in present-day Spain, which still has a contested relationship with its historical memory, riddled with holes and unhealed wounds. In the same way, it is easy to connect this observation of territory with the current upsurge in the Catalan identity movement. But the arguments laid out in these books have more in common with two other aspects. On the one hand—in line with their approach toward everyday life and the present—there is a situation of urban growth and land speculation that has led to an economic and social crisis. Now such themes are present in Catalan literature for the first time. On the other hand, there is also the reality of globalization, of liquid spaces and human migrations and movement which, in Catalonia and Spain came much later than in other parts of Europe and which has had a huge impact on a society which remains highly territorialized.[23] So, there is a contact, obviously, with the Catalan and Spanish political climate, but from a point of view of social and political reflection in a large and fundamental sense, and not from a narrow position or party political discourse.

Thus, we have a border that is both personal and social, that looks at various aspects of social reality: the marginalization and segregation of parts of the population, superficiality and consumerism, memory and oblivion. We have seen that it is also a border of genres and styles. And it is, as we set out at the beginning of this text, a landscape that is physically fragmented, cut up, mixed. Let us look at this place: everything emerges from here, from our place, looked at thoroughly. The physical descriptions of these landscapes match the whole feeling of the border, the experience of the border emanates from the landscape, occupied, forgotten, damaged. The *I* and the *place*, as I have said, are lost and they reveal their loss, their degradation and their anxiety together. We have made the landscape ugly, especially at the border, and this, in turn, causes harm to people. Let us consider some of the descriptions from these books:

> The construction cranes stand out like stakes that mark out the new slice of conquered country land; they are weather vanes indicating the new direction to be taken by the expanding town, the houses and the streets. . . . Along the path to the river, the dimensions diminish little by little and reappear where you least expect it. The barn, the wall or the farmhouse are transformed into semi-detached houses or apartment blocks. There are derelict old buildings that had housed dozens of immigrants and are now piles of rubble.[24]

> The bus crosses a vast extension of olive groves, all the same, all different, hypnotic; there are abandoned farms, soil rankled by weeds and other pieces of land ploughed clean as a ballroom dance floor. There are houses abandoned along the road and, in the distance, you can just make out the farmhouse, *Mas de Barberans*, a light smudge on the dry treeless slope. . . . The bus is suddenly surrounded by factories, furniture showrooms, and then past the hotel, you are there. . . . it is as if you come into the town by the back door.[25]

The characters cannot escape from themselves in this landscape, nor feel carried away by some sublime experience. There are individual and collective points of reference that are more than suspicious. The impression of fragmentation, disarray and instability reigns here. The tension between global interests and human needs clash in the landscape and those who look on discover the story of the defenceless. The speed and scale of the changes to the landscape, as well as the disengagement of the people who live there with the entities that promote such changes,[26] cause a feeling of restlessness, disappointment and loss. Maybe even grief and rage.[27] It is if the habitat "constructed" upon our contemporary landscapes forcefully expels the more dignified humanity; those who are closest to it.

Harshness but also some beauty are found throughout the pages of these three books. All three are brimming with a very forceful poetry, the poetry of intensity, of outbursts, of barrenness, of sweat, wind and skin. This is the beauty of the contemporary border. Beauty is also a dare to see the limit, to feel it; the beauty of the awareness of loss. And for me it is beauty, in the end, because there is courage; because the characters go, despite it all, to the borders of themselves and the borders of place. They go to the limit and the landscape of the limit to find an answer to this crisis that they can see and feel. A voice tells Teresa, the protagonist of *Dies de frontera*, "But you can't just hitchhike home from Els Límits like it was nothing. How far is it back to Figueres? Fifteen kilometres? Maybe somewhere along the way you'll find some clue, a sign that will show you the way to the future."[28] A clue, a sign in the landscape. Maybe there are no clues in the landscape. Or maybe the clues are, for better or worse, the loss in itself, the border itself. And this is where the strength of these books emerges. It is the sense of knowing that there may not be, after all, much sense to be had. Reading these books, you not only notice the disquiet but also the strength. The border is the experience of a landscape, of someone and of a world where everything rubs against and scratches each other, where everything stumbles and where, at the same time, stumbling on, life must continue—but with awareness; with eyes wide open. The border is where we see the limit and learn all these things from it, even if they hurt. We learn that we lose, learn that we forget, learn, as Vincent Pagès puts it at the end of the book, that sometimes, after the border, it can all continue, the same but different. We can see the beauty in the midst of anguish. We can go on with open eyes; however badly it hurts. The beauty and bravery of restlessness.

In these books, it is very clear that the idea of the border that forms the stories is far removed from the idea of a defined line or cut-off point. Everyday experience gives rise to a story in these crumbling places as well. If the story is, as I explained in relation to de Certeau, life and interaction, the border has to be transformed into a place of interaction and lived in. Thus, according to de Certeau, we see that the border changes side thanks to its story. In fact, what dominates is a "logic of ambiguity" that links completely characters' experiences on these narrations: "it 'turns' the frontier into a crossing, and the river into a bridge. It recounts inversions and displacements."[29] The border becomes a "between," a space between two others that combines the form of the demarcation line with continuation and completeness, making this no-man's land an actual place in the full sense of the word.

· The "between" is also the adjective with Joan Nogué describes contemporary landscapes. While I have spoken so far of the border as a specific space, I would like to conclude by talking about it as an example—the clearest and most extreme example—of contemporary landscape. Joan Nogué says if we look at our landscape, we can see clearly that all of it is fragmented, peripheral, complex and hybrid; it is a landscape full of limits and borders.[30] What he is saying, then is that modern man no longer lives in the landscape, but rather, he is always between landscapes, on boundary lines, on borders.[31] If we look carefully at this space, we find our world stripped bare and man revealed. It is a landscape that is not a reference point, a home, a sublime evasion; instead, it is the between and restlessness. It is a landscape or a line through which we might pass unaware, yet further dehumanized; or else a place we look at bravely and read new stories there. The stories of restlessness, the feeling of the border, that also follows the logic of ambiguity of their place, and they are, at the same time, about the loss and the anguish, the brave curiosity, the consciousness and the desire to build. They deal with the wound and with the healing.

The story is possible here and, quite possibily, it can exist as a creator of a new ethics for this aesthetic of the landscape,[32] of new *metaphorai*. This is what Hervé Fischer insists upon when he underlines the contemporary need to find new myths and then suggests the border as a space in which to invent them. He talks of what he calls "peripherism" as follows:

> We suggest considering *peripherism* as the fable that is opposed to
> unitary centralism, as the challenge to hegemonic, metropolitan
> power and as the celebration of difference. Centralism has devalued
> and subjugated the margins of its territory. . . . Rather than depleting
> the periphery, what we propose is to do is reaffirm its richness—not

lateral, but equal. . . . Nowadays it is, after all, possible (perhaps, and only in certain regions of the world) to successfully appraise the advantages that everyone, both city dwellers and periphery dwellers alike, will gain if we reassess and take on board the regional "distancing" inherited historically from military and political power struggles, and respond to the various imperialisms: colonial, national, metropolitan, and counter the perverse political, economic, religious, cultural, intellectual and artistic effects they have wrought. Affirming the value of *peripherism* is to re-centre oneself: each point is, for each one of us in the vast solitude of the cosmos, the potential centre of the planet's surface, the centre of the world. . . . History has taught us that centres are not eternal but shifting. Our contemporary culture celebrates these new positions.[33]

There exists, therefore, a good use to be made of the border against uniformization and impoverishment, alienation. The perverse effects of multiculturalisms, ethnicisms, communitarianisms, tribalisms and dangerous utopias need to be denounced. We advocate, as an antidote, the need to explore differences, to promote dialogue between cultures and identities, without shutting ourselves away in our own, and finally for us all to become *peripherists* and nomads.[34]

To re-locate ourselves and go on. To see who we are and go on. To see the other and go on. To see where we are and go on. This is the border in these stories, and this is the border in our world: a limit and a continuation at the same time. By telling the story of the borders and reaffirming them we can re-centre ourselves as individuals and as a society, at the personal and collective, intimate and external, level. It is all at once desolation, degradation and complete aridness, and thought, observation; more life-affirming, more human and worldlier. It is the border that de Certeau describes and his logic of ambiguity, the *between*. It is curiosity and disquiet, the restlessness of being in the world of the twenty-first century, as Camille de Toledo says in his highly-recommended poetic essay *L'inquétude d'être au monde*,[35] because the restlessness is to see the limit and the movement of everything, to denounce it and make art from it, to refuse it, to put up with it and continue. Movement, advance, criticism. Restlessness. Anguish and projection, this is the beauty of our border. Asserting it. Finding new stories there. Centering ourselves on the border.

MARIA PUIG PARNAU is a PhD student at the University of Girona under the direction of Xavier Pla, and is carrying out research on new landscapes in twenty-first century Catalan narrative, focusing on the feeling between the individual and the landscape and the values of this new imaginary.

NOTES

1. Joan Nogué, *Entre paisajes* (Barcelona: Àmbit, 2009). Especially, on page 120.
2. Michel Collot, *La Pensée-paysage* (Paris: Actes Sud/ESNP, 2011), 11.
3. "Oda a la pàtria" is a poem published by Bonaventura Carles Aribau on 1832 and *Canigó* is an epic poem published by Jacint Verdaguer on 1886.
4. *Solitud* is a novel published on 1909 by Victor Català (pseudonym of Caterina Albert). The most remarkable work of Joquim Ruyra in relation to landscape is *Marines i Boscatges* (Seascapes and woodland scenes; 1903) and, for Josep Pla, we can mention *El carrer Estret* (Narrow street; 1951) or *El quadern gris* (1982). There is an English translation: Josep Pla, *The Gray Notebook*, trans. by Peter Bush (New York Review of Books, 2014).
5. Published in 1988 by Jesús Moncada.
6. Joan Nogué, "Les paraules i els llocs," *Ara* (April 7), 27.
7. The complete references of their books are: Edgar Illas, *Ball de bastons* (Olot: Galerada, 2014); Vicenç Pagès Jordà, *Dies de frontera* (Barcelona: Proa. La Butxaca, 2014); Adrià Pujol, *Escafarlata d'Empordà* (La Bisbal d'Empordà: Edicions Sidillà, 2011) and *Guia sentimental de l'Empordanet* (Barcelona: Edicions 62, 2016); Marta Rojals, *Primavera, estiu, etcètera* (Barcelona: La Magrana, 2011); Toni Sala, *Rodalies* (Barcelona: Edicions 62, 2004), *Marina* (Barcelona: Edicions 62: 2010) and *Els nois* (Barcelona: L'Altra Editorial, 2014); Francesc Serés, *De fems i de marbres* (Barcelona: Quaderns Crema, 2003) and *La pell de la frontera* (Barcelona: Quaderns Crema, 2014); Joan Todó, *L'horitzó primer* (Barcelona: L'Avenç, 2014). The last Toni Sala's book has an English translation: Toni Sala, *The Boys*, Mara Faye, trans. (Two Lines Press, 2015). The last Francesc Serés' book has a Spanish translation: Francesc Serés, *La piel de la frontera*, Nicole d'Amonville Alegría, trans. (Barcelona: Acantilado, 2015). Passages cited in English from these books are translated for this article by Francis Boyle.
8. Michel de Certeau, *The Practice of Everyday Life*, Steven F. Rendall, trans. (Berkeley, Los Angeles, London: University of California Press, 2011 [1974]), 117.
9. Joan Nogué, *Paisatge, territori i societat civil* (València: Tres i Quatre, 2010), 31.
10. Marc Augé, *Non-lieux. Introduction à une anthropologie de la surmodernité* (Paris: Seuil, 2010), 69.

11. Ibid., 68.
12. De Certeau, *The Practice of Everyday Life*, 115.
13. I have provided more or less literal translations of the titles, as there are, to date, no official translations of any of these works.
14. Henri Lefebvre, *La production de l'espace* (Paris: Anthropos, 2000 (1974)), 13–14.
15. Bruce Bégout, *Common Place. The American Motel*, Colin Keaveney, trans. (Los Angeles: Otis Books and Seismicity Editions, 2010), 51.
16. Joan Todó, *L'horitzó primer* (Barcelona: L'Avenç, 2014), 181.
17. Francesc Serés, *La pell de la frontera* (Barcelona: Quaderns Crema), 72–73.
18. Ibid., 72.
19. Bégout, *Common Place. The American Motel*, 118.
20. Todó, *L'horitzó primer*, 96.
21. Vicenç Pagès, *Dies de frontera* (Barcelona: Proa. La Butxaca, 2014). This description is from the impressions given by Vicenç Pagès in the chapter entitled "Publicitat dada" (Dadaist Advertising), 120–124.
22. Ibid., 123–124.
23. Nogué, *Paisatge, territori i societat civil*, 37, 49–56.
24. Serés, *La pell de la frontera*, 60.
25. Todó, *L'horitzó primer*, 18.
26. Nogué, *Paisatge, territori i societat civil*, 42.
27. cf. Francesco Vallerani, " Pèrdua traumàtica del sentit del lloc," *Paisatge i salut* (Olot: Observatori del paisatge, 2008), 52–78.
28. Pagès, *Dies de frontera*, 289.
29. De Certeau, *The Practice of Everyday Life*, 128.
30. I refer particularly to the book, *Entre paisajes* (Between landscapes) (Barcelona: Àmbit, 2009) but also to other press articles and collaborative work such as Joan Nogué, Laura Puigbert, Gemma Bretcha, Àgata Losantos (eds.), *Franges. Els paisatges de la perifèria* (Olot: Observatori del Paisatge de Catalunya, 2012).
31. Nogué, *Entre paisajes*, 103.
32. cf. Jörg Zimmer, "La dimensión ética de la estética del paisaje," *El paisaje en la cultura contemporánea*, Joan Nogué ed. (Madrid: Biblioteca Nueva, 2008), 27–44.
33. Hervé Fischer, "Mitoanàlisi de la frontera," *L'afrontera. De la dominació a l'art de transgredir*, Òscar Jané and Eric Forcada eds. (Catarroja, Figueres, Perpinyà: Editorial Afers, 2011), 51. Translation by Francis Boyle.
34. Ibid., 54.
35. cf. Camille de Toledo, *L'inquiétude d'être au monde* (Paris: Verdier, 2012).

Presence and Pilgrims

Distinguishing the Travelers of the Past

SKYE DONEY

Abstract

This article examines the experiences of pilgrims to Trier between 1844–1933 and argues that pilgrimage is a separate practice from tourism in the nineteenth and early twentieth centuries. Scholars have treated pilgrims like tourists, especially in the twentieth century, but travelers to the Holy Coat of Trier did not think of themselves as tourists. Labeling pilgrim participants as "modern tourists" ignores their religious motivations to travel and creates a false dichotomy between "pilgrims" of the medieval and early modern period and "tourists" of post-Industrial Revolution Europe. Pilgrims who sought a miraculous physical cure or encounter with the blood of Jesus in the Coat of Trier wanted to gain access to divine presence they identified as part of the space of Trier. Pilgrim use of sacred space should lead historians to draw sharper distinctions between the motivations of pilgrims seeking sacred presence and tourists seeking recreation.

INTRODUCTION

Maria Fröhlich traveled from Koblenz to Trier in 1844. As she sailed down the Mosel River, she and her group sang songs about Jesus and the Holy Coat of Trier.[1] Non-pilgrims around her group joined in the singing when they recognized the song.[2] The ship was incorporated into the journey. The moving pilgrim community transformed the trip from Koblenz to Trier with their voices. Their communal activities turned space (the deck of the ship) into place (part of the spiritual preparation to see the Holy Coat in Trier). The singers " 'cosmicize[d]' space and communicate with the transhuman world of heaven."[3] The assembled people in Trier, the participants in processions, and the individuals who sent letters to Church and city officials sacralized profane places as they traveled.[4] Most of the motion toward the Holy Coat of Jesus involved a physical journey, pilgrims proceeded on foot, pedaled bikes, drove cars, and rode in trains. As they moved, pilgrims remade profane spaces into sacred places through their shared actions.[5]

Pilgrims like Maria Fröhlich believed that the Coat was, in fact, imbued with supernatural presence. Historians have focused on the politics of pilgrimage and pilgrim consumption but have overlooked the boundaries of traveler mentalities, including the relationship of European pilgrims to the object at the center of their destination.[6] Pilgrims engaged in a complex pursuit of the sacred that cannot be understood without first examining how individuals related to the sacred objects, like the Trier Holy Coat, at the center of their journey.

Between 1844 and 1933 millions of pilgrims traveled to visit the Holy Coat of Jesus in Trier, Germany. At the center of their travels was the Coat, a brownish-red garment said to have been worn by Jesus during his ministry in Palestine. Because the pilgrimage to Trier took place only once a generation, most visitors in 1844, 1891, and 1933 had never before viewed the Holy Coat. Church officials in Trier had exhibited the relic in infrequent intervals since 1196.[7] The first nineteenth-century pilgrimage, in 1810, drew 227,000 pilgrims and commemorated the return of the relic from Augsburg.[8] Catholic clergy hid the relic throughout Germany—including in the Ehrenbreitstein fortress—during the French Revolution because they feared Revolutionary armies would destroy the garment of Jesus. As part of this seven-hundred-year tradition, in 1844 Trier Bishop Wilhelm Arnoldi called for a pilgrimage to celebrate the peace of Europe and the fact that German Catholicism had survived the revolutions of the early nineteenth century. The period between 1844 and 1933 was the height of Trier pilgrimage attendance. In 1933, over two million pilgrims visited the cathedral and relic. Following World War II, Rhineland pilgrimage attendance entered into a protracted period of declining participation.[9]

Within their correspondence, pilgrims explained to Church authorities that the sacred was simultaneously fixed to the Coat and unbound. Therefore, pilgrims could "be with the Coat" by traveling to the town of Trier, by touching the relic itself, and by holding a secondary object—such as a rosary or a piece of silk—that had been in contact with the relic. This last category allowed individuals far away from Trier, in

Ergolding, in Asia, in the United States to share the space of the Coat during and after the pilgrimages. For pilgrims, the closer one could get, or the closer an object had been, to the relic itself, the nearer one was to being in the presence of the divine. This presence spread out from Trier and reached Catholics around the world.

God's presence, which pilgrims believed to be radiating out of the Holy Coat, was accessible through visiting the relic or via having an object that touched the Coat sent to them at home. When Catholics wrote to clergy and pilgrimage officials, they cited physical proximity— "If only I had a single thread from the Holy Coat!"—as their main reason for traveling to Trier or for writing to Church officials.[10] For instance, some pilgrims embarked on a journey because they expected to encounter Jesus' actual blood at their destination. Pilgrims prepared themselves for meeting the divine within the relic by worshipping during their journey. Like Fröhlich on the deck of a ship, consciously transformed profane spaces into pilgrim places through loud songs and prayers. Through an examination of the correspondence of pilgrims to the Holy Coat of Trier between 1844–1933, this article explores how they understood the Coat to be a place of divine presence. In short, the Coat was a site where the boundary between the temporal and eternal broke down for pilgrims. Individuals both wrote letters and left their homes with the goal of gaining access to this presence in Trier.

Historians must be cautious in discussing forms of travel in nineteenth and twentieth-century Europe.[11] Historians and tourism studies scholars have studied travelers around the world in order to delineate the boundaries between pilgrimage and tourism. This discussion has most often asked whether or not tourism and pilgrimage are in fact the same form of travel. Within the literature, authors focus on traveler motivations in order to place them on a continuum that ranges from sacred (pilgrims) to profane (tourists); from "premodern" to "modern." Currently, the debate has settled into an uneasy stalemate that ultimately views pilgrims after the Industrial Revolution as a subset of modern tourists with both groups completing the same basic activity.

Yet, etymologically and practically, "pilgrimage" and "tourism" indicate unique forms of travel. Pilgrimage/pilgrim is derived from the Latin *peregrinus*, which can mean stranger, foreigner, wanderer, traveler, exile, or even newcomer.[12] Isidore of Seville defined the *peregri-*

nus traveler as "a stranger in a strange land."[13] For St. Augustine, the pilgrim was a "foreigner . . . who want[s] to go home."[14] Conversely, "tourist" is derived from the Latin *tornus*, "an individual who makes a circuitous journey—usually for pleasure—and returns to the starting point."[15] There are unique aspects to completing a pilgrimage that do not neatly correspond with tourism, such as the expectation of individuals writing to clergy in Trier that they would physically encounter God's presence in the Holy Coat of Jesus when they entered the cathedral, or when part of that sacred space was sent to them via silk that had touched the Coat. This hope was an essential aspect of pilgrimage to Trier and helps explain why millions of Europeans traveled to view and touch this fabric relic.

Rather than defining tourism based on perceived motivations, scholars should assess traveling by prioritizing first-hand accounts. In the case of travelers to Trier in the nineteenth and early-twentieth century, the core motivation of encountering the divine presence in the Coat remained consistent. Some aspects of the pilgrimage changed over one hundred years, but the core belief in the physical presence within the Coat remained unchanged. That consistency is remarkable considering the significant shifts in German culture and society concurrent with this period of time. Pilgrims oriented themselves towards the past, towards the narratives of the New Testament, and towards an object that was for them part of Jesus' life. Even as they adapted nominally modern technologies—trains, telephones, electric lighting—to their practices, they looked to the generations of previous pilgrims who had made similar journeys away from home and who had moved in the direction of sacred presence. This was not tourism according to the conventional theoretical scholarly conceptualization.

THE PROBLEMS OF MOTIVATION

Maria Fröhlich traveled to Trier because she believed the Coat provided access to Jesus. She participated in a form of Christian devotion that developed in the first centuries after Constantine legalized Christianity in 311. Christian pilgrimage emerged from two distinct traveling groups in the Roman world. First, monastic pilgrims, individuals who constantly moved from place to place and lived out the asceticism of

Christian homelessness.[16] The second group, comprised of former Roman empresses, made circular trips and journeyed in lavish groups, establishing holy places along their routes.[17] The most famous of these, St. Helena, Constantine's mother, built and organized monasteries and churches in Palestine and Europe. St. Helena also donated her Trier home to the bishop, who used it to build a cathedral. Early Christians thus took to the road for a variety of reasons; for penance to cleanse sins, for healing, to convert those they met, and out of piety.[18] This multiplicity of religious motivations is shared by pilgrims in the nineteenth and twentieth centuries.

Scholars have misunderstood pilgrims who pursue divine presence. They have turned pilgrims into tourists both by overemphasizing economic practices and by building up their analyses on the foundations of Mircea Eliade and Victor Turner. From Eliade, scholars appropriated the "sacred center" as a means of distinguishing forms of travel. In 2003, Justine Digance turned to Eliade to make sense of why people traveled to the Uluru rock in Australia. Here she concluded that contemporary travelers complete "secular pilgrimages." Increasing interest in Uluru and Stonehenge in England indicated how traditionally profane places can be made sacred over time.[19] Digance's "secular pilgrims" borrowed from both "religious and tribal traditions." Scholars have tried to meld Eliade's hierarchical approach to sacred practices onto a methodology that requires beginning with traveling laity: the tourists. The result has been confusion and classification chaos.[20]

Unsatisfied with analyses of travel that completely excluded religious journeys, Victor Turner examined pilgrimages across time and religion, from pre-Christian Europe to early Buddhism, from ancient Egypt to Malcolm X's 1964 hajj to Mecca.[21] From Turner, scholars acquired a new vocabulary—"communitas," "out there," "liminal"—to describe the experience of religious travelers. As a group, pilgrims created a sense of shared purpose through their mutual destination: "communitas." Whether existential, ideological, or normative, communitas overcame national, political, and social boundaries between pilgrims by uniting them in a common goal. The sacred center varied by region and faith, from major cathedrals in the center of European cities to peripheral shrines in rural Mexico. Scholars also borrowed transition metaphors from Turner. The pilgrim moved across a limin or "a place and moment 'in and out of time.'"[22] The limin distinguishes *authentic* pilgrims, who are part of spiritual societies, and *modern* travelers who originate in materialistic societies.

Turner's liminal vs. liminoid, simple vs. complex distinctions relied heavily on Weber and Calvin. Through Weber, Turner argued that industrial societies push the liminal into the liminoid.[23] Only agrarian societies experienced authentic crossing-over experiences. In "primitive," "tribal," and "simpler" societies, those that developed before the Industrial Revolution, the liminal was most frequently found via a rite of passage.[24] Conversely, Turner explains that after the Industrial Revolution, the West transformed the liminal into forms of leisure: arts, novels, paintings, etc.[25] The pilgrim, by moving toward the pilgrimage center, traveled to a border, moved past a threshold into a space and moment both "in and out of time," where they could directly experience "the sacred, invisible, or supernatural order."[26] "Complex" societies pushed the liminal into liminoid experiences, which occurred in leisure settings like the café, bar, or social club.[27] Turner, despite providing scholars with new categories to understand the spatial significance of religious journeys, pulled back and labeled liminal boundaries and communitas as essentially pre-modern phenomena.[28] Pilgrimage had no place in the modern world (West) as a serious venture, but had contributed a "pilgrim ethic" (presumably to complement Weber's Protestant "work ethic") that developed a "communications net[work] that later made capitalism a viable national and international system."[29] Turner thus asserted the importance of myth and transcendence for pilgrims, but concluded that this is not part of a post-Industrial worldview.[30] Yet, pilgrims from the Rhineland continued to pursue the spiritual center(s) of Rhenish Catholicism long after the French Revolution or Weber's *Protestant Work Ethic*.[31] The "primitive" liminal argument cannot account for the recurrence of major Catholic pilgrimages in the Rhineland, next door to the industrial heartland of Germany, the Ruhr.

Turner's vocabulary provided a means with which to evaluate travel in terms of societal "development." Rituals, including travel, varied according to the technological advancement of a culture, "[n]on-industrial societies tend to stress immediate context-sensitive ritual; industrial pre-electronic societies tend to stress theatre."[32] In pilgrimage, Turner's view of progress translated into two types of pilgrimage destinations. In the first, the "center" is a political or ancestral location. Turner situated these spaces in West and Central Africa. Conversely, centers that stressed "the general good and inclusiveness" are located "in the so-called historical, higher, or universal religions such as Christianity, Judaism, Buddhism, Islam, Confucianism, and Hinduism."[33] For Turner, the ideal conditions for pilgrimage to flourish were "societies based mainly on agriculture, but with a fairly advanced degree of division of craft labor, with patrimonial or feudal political regimes, with a well-marked urban-rural division but with, at the most, only a limited development of modern industry."[34] It is little surprise that scholars have replicated Turner's modern/premodern or authentic/inauthentic measurement for the boundaries between pilgrimage and tourism. Accordingly, pilgrimage has been historically superseded and to the extent that we can still observe it in practice the modern touristic elements drown out trace elements of an agricultural society's formalized rituals. Despite all of the varied typologies of travel, scholars continue to affirm Turner's binaries: advanced vs. primitive societies, religion vs. premodern superstition, even sacred (pilgrimage) vs. profane (tourism). Pilgrimage thus comes from within the (premodern) traveler. In part this is because scholars combine current modes of analyzing tourist motivations even as they concede that *desire* is a fickle factor and difficult to quantify.

Scholars have built on Eliade and Turner in order to understand the relationship of pilgrimage to tourism and to demarcate the border between modern forms of travel for leisure and earlier religiously-motivated journeys. Initially distinguishing pilgrims from tourists was seemingly straightforward. Tourists were those modern individuals who sought either pseudo-events or authentic spaces. In Daniel Boorstin's model, travelers did not want to actually leave behind the comforts of home, but pursued the illusion of having an exotic experience.[35] Conversely, Dean MacCannell asserted that tourists desired access to "backstage" areas such as kitchens. They wanted to see how people actually lived.[36] Regardless of whether the traveler sought out a "real" experience or not, both Boorstin and MacCannell agreed that the contemporary traveler was inherently a tourist in pursuit of diversion and not a pilgrim. Early studies thus conceptualized tourism as replacing pilgrimage by creating the illusion of authenticity. Modern travelers realized there were no real experiences and readily accepted artificial versions in their pursuit of diversionary activities.

By the 1970s, scholars moved away from the Boorstin/MacCannell authenticity debate but continued to exclude pilgrims in their increasingly complex models for tracking traveler motivations. In 1974, Erik Cohen urged scholars to develop an analytical distinction between the "tourist" and other travelers. He outlined, for instance, the "experimental pilgrim" as a person who does "not adhere any more to the spiritual centre of their own society, but engage[s] in a quest for an alternative in many different directions"[37] The modern pilgrims were all who left home in pursuit of meaning outside their own society or "center." For Cohen, people traveled for "superficial," "profound," "recreational," "diversionary," "experiential," "experimental," and "existential" reasons.[38] In each case, the individual sought to move away from the center of society toward the periphery. The closest approximation to a pilgrim here is the existential traveler. Cohen understood the pursuit of an authentic, sacred experience to also be a "leisure activity" that fell within the parameters of modern tourism. Ultimately, Cohen defined a tourist as a "voluntary, temporary traveler, traveling in the expectation of pleasure from the novelty and change experienced on a relatively long and non-recurrent round-trip."[39] This conception again excludes Rhineland pilgrims like Fröhlich who did not embark on an unusually long journey. But, more problematically, Cohen conceptualized "pilgrims" as "part-time tourists," who participated in "a form of 'religious tourism'"[40] There is no room here for individuals traveling for purposes other than to have a holiday.

In response to Cohen's typological models, scholars continued to establish traveler classifications that excluded pilgrims through the 1980s and into the 1990s. The range of rubrics, requirements, parameters, and survey groupings is staggering. Donald Redfoot identified four types of travelers based on the "reality experiences" of the individual. He ranked his ideal types into four "orders" each progressively more interested in understanding reality via travel. Only the fourth group, "spiritual tourists," were interested in making a form of pilgrimage. And these, Redfoot explained, tended to be middle-class individuals from the west pursuing spirituality "in experiences of other traditions."[41] For Redfoot, there were no "pilgrims" because touristic authenticity was only possible when an individual felt a profound alienation from their home world.[42] Tom Selwyn expanded Redfoot's methodology by combining the perspectives of tourists, locals, and observers of tourists. Selwyn distinguished a range of authenticity: from "hot" to "cool." "Hot" authenticity was mediated by the emotions. The traveler "felt" that a travel destination or artifact was real. In contrast, third parties such as museum curators and tour guides conveyed "cool" authenticity. In both hot and cool evaluations, the traveler is gullible or unstable. Tourists thought that places and objects were legitimate because they were told so by experts. Hot and cool authenticity, while helpful in moving the discussion beyond travelers as consumers, began with tourism and assumed that modern travel is essentially the "invention and reinvention of tradition."[43]

In the 1990s and 2000s historians and tourism studies scholars increasingly examined European pilgrimages after the French Revolution. They expanded on motivation as the key signifier of traveler types to include habits, or what individuals did when they were on journeys.[44] Suzanne Kaufman found that modern consumption practices in Lourdes, France permanently transformed a sacred space into a touristic destination, "the rise of consumer culture during this period transformed the act of pilgrimage into an early form of tourism characterized by inexpensive church-organized voyages and the buying and selling of mass-produced goods."[45] Kaufman criticized MacCannell and subsequent arguments based on his theory of authenticity for not addressing how pilgrimage changed in response to consumption. The Lourdes shrine was profitable and succeeded because of contemporary advertising techniques. Visitors were taught not only how to be good pilgrims but how to consume the shrine.[46] Ultimately, for Kaufman, pilgrimage and tourism were nearly indistinguishable at Lourdes. She urged historians to examine the interrelationship of pilgrimage and tourism as historical constructs. Kaufman is part of a larger trend among scholars to view pilgrims throughout history as proto-tourists. For instance, Justine Digance echoed Jonathan Sumption's 1975 description of medieval pilgrims as the tourists of their day.[47]

Like tourism, scholars have classified and reclassified "pilgrimage" following the MacCannell/Boorstin debate. Robert Stoddard criticized motivation as an untrustworthy rubric. Travelers did not always know why they embarked on a journey. Their reasons for travel were fickle and easily changed. After outlining twenty-seven forms of pilgrimage, he offered as a definition: "an event consisting of longer than local journeys by numerous persons to a sacred place as an act of religious devotion."[48] For Stoddard, pilgrimages are thus best grouped according to three characteristics: length of journey, frequency of the event, and route pilgrims follow. Each of these in turn had several sub-categories. Frequency, for instance, included frequent, annual, and rare groupings. Pilgrimage here is best analyzed in terms of time, distance, and form. By shifting focus away from perceptions, Stoddard urged scholars to ask new questions of pilgrimage destinations. European historians followed, Raymond Jonas in his analysis of Sacré Cœur classified pilgrimage as "voyage to a holy place," for example.[49]

Even with scholarly focus shifting to destination over traveler motivation, researchers continue to analyze pilgrims as a form of tourist. Aliza Fleischer, in her study of pilgrims and tourists in the Holy Land found that, "Christian pilgrims to the Holy Land have evolved over the years into tourists."[50] Fleischer excavated the "tourist" within the "pilgrim" among travelers to the Holy Land. She uncovered the innermost identity of the traveler by examining their most visible practices, including how much travelers spent on souvenirs and how long they stayed in the Holy Land. Accordingly, pilgrims spend less on lodging, but more on memorabilia to commemorate their journey. Fleischer grounded her evolutionary understanding of travelers in consumption practices as both groups spent money while in the Holy Land.

Pilgrims who sought a physical cure or encounter with the blood of Jesus in the Coat of Trier do not fit easily into current conceptions of travelers. By listening to the voices of the travelers to Trier between 1844–1933 it quickly becomes apparent that pilgrimage continued long after the Industrial and French Revolutions and includes individuals that did not actually travel to see the Coat. The participants did not see themselves as tourists with a modern hierophany, whether frivolity, escapism, consumption, or movement away from the center.[51] Instead, many described the ways in which God was to be found at their destination. By discussing the expectations of individual pilgrims below, I propose that historians and tourism studies scholars begin their analyses with individual travelers rather than by trying to unmask the contemporary tourist beneath the pilgrim. Instead of asking how pilgrimage turn into modern tourism, we should ask how has pilgrimage endured even after the rise of mass tourism. Pilgrims continued to make difficult journeys towards holy relics, long after the proposed transition from pilgrim to tourist in the late eighteenth century; there are striking continuities within Christian pilgrimage practices that extend into the twentieth century.

THE PRIMACY OF PRESENCE

On April 19, 1937, Maria Schwemmhuber, who lived in Ergolding, wrote to Trier Bishop Franz Rudolf Bornewasser, to ask for a piece of a sacred relic, "[i]f only I had a single thread from the Holy Coat! Then I might be well again!" Schwemmhuber suffered from severe stomach pains. She had been praying constantly for relief but so far her pleas had gone unanswered. The family's situation was desperate. Since December 1936 her husband had also been sick, which put the Schwemmhubers in a precarious economic position. "everywhere distress and misery, we live in a rented apartment . . . almost twenty years of pain without end; please, please help us through prayer."[52] Two days later, Vicar General Heinrich Hubert Ludwig von Meurers, one of Bishop Bornewasser's clergy, sent the family a piece of silk that had wrapped the Holy Coat of Jesus between 1891 and 1933.[53] The Trier clergy could not send the Schwemmhuber family an actual piece of the Holy Coat. They had sealed the relic in 1933 at the close of the last pilgrimage and would not open the reliquary again until 1959.

Trier correspondents, like Maria Schwemmhuber, traveled not for diversion but to meditate on pain, on sacrifice, and the fact that life is fleeting and death inevitable. The songs pilgrims sang out on ships and trains stressed the physical presence of Christ and God in the relics. Their lyrics included: "This Coat clothed you, Redeemer of men," "At the familiar place the God-man prays in grief, "Without rest Jesus moved from country to country in the Coat spreading his divine word and heavenly seeds," and "there [his] bloody sweat flows through this garment."[54] The songs evoked sacrifice, journey, and Jesus' physical nature. Blood flowing into the Trier Coat was a common theme of songs, "the blood . . . from the scourge wounds was absorbed by your holy threads,"[55] "The Coat is sprinkled with blood," and "In this Coat my Lord and God, you suffered bitter distress, hunger."[56] The relic was worthy of visitation and meditation because it contacted Christ's body and contained intimate traces of the divine: Jesus' blood and his tears.

Pilgrims were often physically overwhelmed when they finally reached the Holy Coat; they cried out and wept as they neared the goal of their destination. "The attitude of the pilgrims was most edifying," wrote one priest about his parish traveling from Aachen to Trier in 1891, "[i]n some eyes of pious worshiper[s] glistened tears of emotions."[57] Another visitor to Trier wrote down that "on the 10th of September at Mass I observed an individual who held a picture of the Holy Coat and was full of devotion. He repeatedly wiped tears from his eyes."[58] In 1933, Father Mayer in Zimming wrote on behalf of Frl. Zimmer, "with tears in her eyes, [she] wishes to be allowed to touch the Holy Coat of the Redeemer."[59] Pilgrims did not travel solely for recreation or to purchase objects; they were desperate to get to their destination and the promise of a transcendent encounter in the space of the Holy Coat.[60]

Sick pilgrims hoped that by touching the Holy Coat they would experience something otherwise impossible: sudden and complete physical healing; spiritual renewal; or familial conversion.[61] Twenty-one-year-old Maria Sibilla Müller from Noswendel was one of thousands of pilgrims who traveled to the Holy Coat in hope of a miracle. Over Christmas 1842, her right hand began to hurt and the pain spread through her body. Her condition deteriorated into the spring of 1843. By Easter, Müller could no longer knit and getting out of bed brought on painful cramps. When she arrived in Trier on Friday, 13 September 1844, her arms were weak and distorted by gout. Müller slowly approached the Holy Coat and with the help of two guards was only able to extend her arm far enough to brush the Coat with the tips of her fingers. She immediately fell backwards into the arms of an honorary guard. She then cried out a loud prayer in which she praised the Coat that contained the blood of Jesus and fainted for fifteen minutes. When she awoke she reported that her arms were healed and exited the church.[62]

Not all pilgrimage in the Rhineland involved physical travel or directly touching the Holy Coat of Jesus. German pilgrims made both direct and indirect journeys to Trier further suggesting that the promise of presence transcends the pilgrim/tourist dichotomy. They participated by writing letters, by praying, and having part of the sacred sent to them.[63] This type of travel was not literal movement but completed when pilgrims, including the Schwemmhubers, received items that physically touched the Coat; these objects contained the sacred space of the relic. Dom Jean LeClerq describes this as *peregrinatio in stabilitate* (stable pilgrimage) traveling with the heart and not with the feet.[64] Medieval monks used their imaginations to make texts both historically and spatially "present," argues LeClerq.[65] For monks, the past was "not . . . definitely over, but . . . a living reality which continued to animate the present."[66] Sacred texts allowed the reader to visit ancient or contemporary Jerusalem or to travel to heaven without leaving the monastery. St. Bernard of Clairvaux discussed how monks could find the Heavenly Jerusalem within the cloister without leaving Europe for Palestine.[67] *Peregrinatio in stabilitate* was not just a medieval concept, however. In Trier, far-flung individuals were active, not just discursive pilgrim participants in the events.[68]

Emma Figulla, for instance, wrote to Trier pilgrimage officials in 1933 from Ratibor in Silesia. She asked them to touch a golden ring to the Holy Coat. The ring had belonged to her deceased father. Since his death Emma had worn it. For the previous nine years Emma suffered from an unnamed bone, joint, and tendon disease. She was exhausted and did not have the strength to personally attend the Trier event. Emma heard an inner voice reminding her of her father's ring and urging her to send it on to Trier. After a period of relative strength, she acted on this interior urge and sent the ring. "God can heal me from a distance," wrote Emma, "as he healed the servant of the centurion Cornelius."[69] Emma referenced the centurion in Matthew 8:8–9 who told Jesus: "Lord, I do not deserve to have you come under my roof. But just say the word, and my servant will be healed. For I myself am a man under authority, with soldiers under me. I tell this one, 'Go,' and he goes; and that one, 'Come,' and he comes. I say to my servant, 'Do this,' and he does it." In response to the Centurion's statement of faith Jesus healed his servant from where he stood without traveling back home with the Roman and his soldiers. Emma sent her father's ring out of faith, along with stamps so that it could be returned. While she could not personally attend the pilgrimage, Emma did not believe this in any way diminished her participation. The ring acted as a surrogate pilgrim for Emma. Her father's ring could touch the Coat for her, make the circuitous journey, and bring divine presence back to her in Ratibor. Pilgrim letters like Emma's illustrate what value the relics held for pilgrims even when literal travel was impossible to complete.

Similarly, Rosina Benitz wrote to the Trier Bishop Felix Michael Korum in 1891. Benitz explained that she was in constant pain. She suffered from headaches that kept her up all night. They had begun forty-three years earlier in 1848. For the past thirty years she had eye troubles. On top of these maladies, Benitz was troubled by gastritis and jaw pain for the past year. "I am completely alone, widow without children."[70] She was not without hope: "I have read that in 1844 when the Holy Coat was displayed that there were many miracles through images that had been touched to the Holy Coat."[71] Reports of miracles had been widely publicized during the 1844 pilgrimage. Benitz now lived in Erie, Pennsylvania in the United States. She did not have the financial resources to take a ship across the Atlantic to visit the Coat. Even so, she wanted to participate. In her letter, she asked Trier Bishop Felix Michael Korum to select 2–3 "small pictures" of the Holy Coat and press them against the relic before sending them to her in Pennsylvania. There was divine presence in the Coat that could overcome the limitations of Benitz's body and make her well. The images would act for Benitz. After touching the Coat they would be filled with sacred presence. She stressed again the fact that the relic needed to touch the three small images before the bishop sent them back. On the last page of her note, Benitz explained that once she had the images she would give one to a sick friend. They planned to put them into water and drink them. They would ingest the embodied divine presence to change their bodies. This was not tourism, but pilgrimage to presence, and ingesting the sacred space of Trier.

Müller and Benitz are emblematic of the promise of presence. Müller believed that the droplets of blood within the relic would connect her to the body of Jesus and relieve her constant suffering. Pilgrimage is in part movement toward a place where God becomes "really real" and is present.[72] As Robert Orsi argued, scholars must acknowledge "the reality of the Catholic supernatural" when discussing Catholic rites and practices. Catholic pilgrims to Trier intended to have an encounter with Jesus via the Holy Coat. In Europe in the nineteenth and twentieth centuries thousands of individuals held similar hope as Maria Sibilla Müller as they made their way towards sacred centers in Lourdes, Fatima, Knox, Marpingen, and dozens of other national and regional sites of sacred significance. In their hope to commune with the dead and with God they thought of themselves as participants in a sacred community, not as tourists hoping for an existential experience, but as pilgrims toward an eternal city.

CONCLUSION

The "center" held special significance not because of a communal spirit generated by traveling but because the divine was accessible at the site of the Holy Coat. Sacred presence permeates pilgrim correspondence and activity in nineteenth- and twentieth-century Germany. Pilgrims made long and short, national, international and local journeys because of the real presence pilgrims believed could be found in Trier.[73] Presence also meant that pilgrims were unfettered by geographic boundaries. Their journey did not begin upon walking out the door. Nor did it end upon returning home from "out there." Rather, pilgrimage is best understood as the active pursuit of sacred presence. This activity consists of three aspects. First, for participants, the mode of travel is irrelevant because authentic, divine presence can cover distances and go to an individual. In other words, it is accessible even if a participant is unable to make the journey. Second, presence transforms public space into sacred place. Finally, for participants, the pursuit of divine presence overcomes the barriers of death, sickness, and even religious creed.

Pilgrimage is a spatially and historically unique ritual. The correspondents to Trier officials between 1844 and 1933 described their need to be near the sacred presence within the Holy Coat. As pilgrims traveled, touched the Coat, or sent proxy objects they viewed themselves as connecting physically to Jesus' body. Travelers explained *why* they wanted to visit holy centers like Trier. By listening closely to pilgrim concerns about their health, their society, and their dead, scholars can better understand why Europeans pursued sacred sites, why they went on pilgrimage, and how religious practices continued to thrive into the twentieth century.

When Emma Figulla wrote her letter and when Maria Sibilla Müller left home they understood themselves to be pilgrims to divine presence in the Holy Coat of Trier. Müller experienced pain as she traveled and it was difficult for her to get to Trier. Figulla could not complete the journey but hoped to still be physically connected to the blood in the Coat through her father's ring. There were many forms of pilgrimage to the Coat of Trier between 1844 and 1933. Scholars have noted that the best way to distinguish travelers is to ask them why they are on the road. Yet, contemporary analyses of tourists and pilgrims have lacked a theoretical framework for understanding the transcendent hopes of individuals like Maria Fröhlich. Her journey is more akin to the "medieval pilgrims" scholars have described as the tourists of their day. By further considering how pilgrims understood their connection or their potential connection to relics and sacred destinations scholars will better understand the continuities of pilgrimage. Presence can nuance Turner's historical dichotomies and push scholars to ask new questions about the pilgrims of the recent past and how religious practices endured through and adapted to the nineteenth and twentieth centuries.

SKYE DONEY is the director at the George L. Mosse Program in European and Jewish History (mosseprogram.wisc.edu). His book manuscript is titled *Moving Toward the German Sacred: Pilgrimage Space, 1832–1937,* and he has published in *International Journal of Religious Tourism and Pilgrimage* and *Catholic Historical Review.*

NOTES

This article was possible through funding from the German Academic Exchange Program (DAAD) and George L. Mosse Program in History. Thanks to Sean Bloch, David Harrisville, Daniel Hummel, John Suval, John Tortorice, Kevin Walters, and the two anonymous reviewers for their feedback and advice.

1. BATr, Abt. 91, Nr. 230a, 18. BATr indicates the Bistumsarchiv Trier in Trier, Germany.
2. BATr, Abt. 91, Nr. 230, 85–39, "bald sangen sie heilig[e] Lieder. Einer aus ihrer, ein angesehene Bürger, sich des Gebet oder dem Gesang an, und die übrigen nahmen ab."
3. Jonathan Z. Smith, *To Take Place: Toward Theory in Ritual* (Chicago: University of Chicago Press, 1992), 2.
4. Esther Allen posits that the traveler's quest for "authenticity" might have been

manufactured by guidebooks themselves because, for travelers, connecting to the genuine experience often meant going off of the scripted path provided in a little red Baedeker or Murray book, " 'Money and little red books': Romanticism, Tourism, and the Rise of the Guidebook," *LIT* 7 (1996): 213–226. Gisbert Rinschede has brought tourism and pilgrimage together in a continuum (pilgrims, tourists, and pilgrim-tourists), but does not offer a compelling differentiation between these three groups. For example, he writes that pilgrims to Fátima were primarily "pure pilgrims," but this assertion is based on the fact that there is little to do around Fátima besides visiting the apparition site, "The Pilgrimage Center of Fatima/ Portugal," in *Pilgrimage in World Religions: Presented to Prof. Dr. Angelika Sievers on the Occasion of her 75th Birthday*, eds. Surinder M. Bhardwaj and Gisbert Rinschede (Berlin: Dietrich Reimer, 1998), 65–98.

5. Michel de Certeau, *The Practice of Everyday Life*, trans. Steven Rendall (Berkeley: University of California Press, 1984), 117. Place, for de Certeau, is stable, "an instantaneous configuration of positions" and is passive. People turn place into space, for example, a street "is transformed into a space by walkers." Space can become place by "the awakening of inert objects," including people. Pilgrims were not unmoving beings before they set out to see relics. Geographers use "place" and "landscape" to discuss cultures.

6. For a political approach see, David Blackbourn, *Marpingen: Apparitions of the Virgin Mary in Nineteenth-Century Germany* (New York: Alfred A. Knopf, 1994).

7. Jakob Marx, *History of the Robe of Jesus Christ: Preserved in the Cathedral of Tréves* (New York: Saxton & Miles, 1845), 27.

8. Erich Aretz, Michael Embach, Martin Persch, Franz Ronig, *Der Heilige Rock zu Trier: Studien zur Geschichte und Verehrung der Tunika Christi* (Trier: Paulinus-Verlag, 1995), 221.

9. In 1959 Trier held the first post-war pilgrimage and pilgrim emphasis on the presence of the relic declined as did attendance to less than half of the 1933 Trier attendance. Bishop Bornewasser selected 1933 for a pilgrimage because it was the thousand-year anniversary of the death of Christ. The event was already being coordinated before Hitler became chancellor on 30 January 1933.

10. BATr, Abt. 90, Nr. 132, 19 April 1937.

11. Rudy Koshar, *German Travel Cultures* (Oxford: Berg, 2000), 15.

12. Noga Collins-Kreiner, Nurit Kliot, Yoel Mansfeld, and Keren Sagi, *Christian Tourism to the Holy Land: Pilgrimage during Security Crisis* (Burlington, Vt.: Ashgate Publishing, 2006), 8; Smith, *To Take Place*, 1.

13. Linda Ellis and Frank. L. Kidner eds., *Travel, Communication and Geography in Late Antiquity: Sacred and Profane* (Burlington, Vt.: Ashgate Publishing, 2004), 126.

14. Ellis and Kidner, *Travel*, 111.

15. Smith, *To Take Place*, 1.

16. Ellis and Kidner, *Travel*, 126.

17. Noel Lanski, "Empresses in the Holy Land: The Creation of a Christian Utopia in Late Antique Palestine," in Ellis and Kidner, *Travel*, 114–124. The Christian taboo on divorce conflicted with the Emperors' habit of abandoning their wives. Empresses who were out of favor with the emperor had good reason to travel away from the capitol, toward the boundaries of the Roman Empire.

18. Susanna Elm, "Perceptions of Jerusalem Pilgrimage as Reflected in Two Early Sources on Female Pilgrimage (3rd and 4th centuries A.D.)," *Studia patristica* 20 (1987): 219–223; Brouria Bitton-Ashkelony, *Encountering the Sacred: The Debate on Christian Pilgrimage in Late Antiquity* (Los Angeles: University of California Press, 2005); Susan Harvey and David G. Hunter eds., *The Oxford Handbook of Early Christian Studies* (Oxford: Oxford University Press, 2008).
19. Justine Digance, "Pilgrimage at Contested Sites." *Annals of Tourism Research* 30, no. 1 (2003): 143–159. See Susan Rosa and Dale Van Kley's caution to historians about using too much theory to explain and understand religion, "Religion and the Historical Discipline: A Reply to Mack Holt and Henry Heller," *French Historical Studies* 21, no. 4 (1998): 611–629.
20. Randall Studstill, "Eliade, Phenomenology, and the Sacred," *Religious Studies* 36, no. 2 (2000): 177–194, 184.
21. Victor Turner, *Dramas, Fields, and Metaphors: Symbolic Action in Human Society* (Ithaca: Cornell University Press, 1974), 197. For Roy Rappaport, ritual helps to bind the community together, *Ecology, Meaning, and Religion* (Richmond, Calif.: North Atlantic Books, 1979).
22. Turner, *Dramas, Fields, and Metaphors*, 197.
23. Victor Turner, "The Center Out There: Pilgrim's Goal," *History of Religions* 12, no. 3 (1973): 191–230, 215; *Dramas, Fields, and Metaphors*, 188; "Liminal to Liminoid, In Play, Flow, and Ritual: An Essay in Comparative Symbology," *Rice University Studies* 60, no. 3 (Summer 1974): 53–94, 70. Recently Christian Smith has urged scholars to view the secularization of the American academy as a revolution. Smith examines early sociology textbooks to show how sociologists discredited religion by reducing it to social utility, see *The Secular Revolution: Power, Interests, and Conflict in the Secularization of American Public Life* (Berkeley: University of California Press, 2003). See also Brad Gregory's argument that the Protestant Reformation led to secularization, *The Unintended Reformation: How a Religious Revolution Secularized Society* (Cambridge, Mass.: Belknap Press of Harvard University Press, 2012), 25–73.
24. Turner, "Liminal to Liminoid," 72.
25. Turner, *Dramas, Fields, and Metaphors*, 208. Turner cites Belgian ethnographer van Gennep as influencing his use of liminality, 196.
26. Turner, *Dramas, Fields, and Metaphors*, 197.
27. Turner, "Liminal to Liminoid," 86.
28. Turner, *Dramas, Fields, and Metaphors*, 228.
29. Turner "The Center Out There," 228. On the topic of Protestant theology and Weber's work ethic, see Friedrich Wilhelm Graf, "The German Theological Sources and Protestant Church Politics," in *Weber's Protestant Work Ethic: Origins, Evidence, Contexts*, eds. Hartmut Lehmann, Guenther Roth (Washington, DC: Cambridge University Press, 1993), 27–49.
30. In his study, Turner reified Eliade's study of aboriginal sacred centers. Eliade conceptualized the sacred in terms of "hierophany," which could be mediated by any object deemed sacred by a religious practitioner. Thus, sacrality was constructed in the mind of a believer. Studstill, "Eliade, Phenomenology, and the Sacred." Jonathan Smith has explored Eliade's *Patterns in Comparative Religion* and argued that Eliade cannot account for human experience with his notions of "history"

and "religion" in "Acknowledgements: Morphology and History in Mircea Eliade's 'Patterns in Comparative Religion' (1949–1999), Part 2: The Texture of the Work," *History of Religions* 39, no. 4 (2000): 332–351.

31. The geographer Gisbert Rinschede argued that travelers to Lourdes, France were touristic because of their interaction with the built environment. For Rinschede, like tourist attractions, Lourdes structures were "used mostly on a seasonal basis, ha[d] surplus facilities in the off season and it [was] accessible by various means of transportation." Structurally there was no notable difference between a site made popular for touristic or pilgrim purposes. Any differences between the Lourdes pilgrim and tourist resulted "primarily from the visitors' goals and from the specific activities of the social groups in a given space." See "The Pilgrimage Town of Lourdes," *Journal of Cultural Geography* 7, no. 1 (1986): 21–34, 33.

32. Victor Turner, "Are There Universals of Performance in Myth, Ritual and Drama," in *By Means of Performance: Intercultural Studies of Theatre and Ritual*, eds. Richard Schechner and Willa Appel (New York: Cambridge University Press, 1990: 8–18, 8.

33. Turner, "The Center Out There," 207.

34. Turner, "The Center Out There," 195. See also Victor Turner and Edith Turner, "Postindustrial Marian Pilgrimage," in *Mother Worship: Theme and Variations*, ed. Preston James (Chapel Hill: University of North Carolina Press, 1982): 145–173.

35. Daniel Boorstin, *The Image: A Guide to Pseudo-Events in America* (Magnolia, Mass.: Peter Smith, 1985), 77.

36. Dean MacCannell, "Staged Authenticity: Arrangements of Social Space in Tourist Settings," *American Journal of Sociology* 79, no. 3 (1973): 589–603.

37. Erik Cohen, "Who is a Tourist?: A Conceptual Clarification," *Sociological Review* 22, no. 4 (1974): 527–555, 533. Graham M.S. Dann defines tourist motivation as, "A meaningful state of mind which adequately disposes an actor or group of actors to travel, and which is subsequently interpretable by others as a valid explanation for such a decision," "Tourist Motivation: An Appraisal," *Annals of Tourism Research* 8, no. 2 (1981): 187–219. Donald L. Redfoot proposes four orders of tourists: true tourist, angst-ridden tourist, anthropological tourist, and spiritual tourist, "Touristic Authenticity, Touristic Angst, and Modern Reality," *Qualitative Sociology* 7, no. 4 (1984): 291–309. Elery Hamilton-Smith proposes four kinds of tourism based on structural and existential dimensions, "Four Kinds of Tourism?," *Annals of Tourism Research* 14 (1987): 332–344. Bryan Pfaffenberger has shown that in Sri Lanka pilgrim motivations can be just as diverse as tourist motivations and include frivolity and superficiality, "Serious Pilgrims and Frivolous Tourists: The Chimera of Tourism in the Pilgrimages of Sri Lanka," *Annals of Tourism Research* 19 (1992): 57–74. See also Alan Goldberg's work on Haitian voodoo shows for a discussion of participant motivation, "Identity and Experience in Haitian Voodoo Shows," *Annals of Tourism Research* 10 (1983): 479–495.

38. Erik Cohen, "A Phenomenology of Tourist Experiences," *Sociology* 13 (1979): 179–201, 183.

39. Cohen, "Who is a Tourist?, 533.

40. Erik Cohen, "Tourism and Religion: A Comparative Perspective," *Pacific Tourism Review* 2 (1998): 1–10, 1. Yet, for Cohen, "religious tourism," as it came to be used

to describe travel to religious sites, was not useful because he wanted to maintain the distinction between "existential" and "experimental" tourists. He agreed with MacCannell and Turner that "modern pilgrims" were actually tourists and should be studied as such, "Who is a Tourist?," 542.

41. Redfoot, "Touristic Authenticity," 301.

42. See also Judith Adler, "interpret meanings that travel performances hold for practitioners and their publics to show the relationship between these meanings and other social practices," "Travel as Performed Art," *American Journal of Sociology* 94, no. 6 (1989): 1366–1391, 1382.

43. Tom Selwyn ed., *The Tourist Image: Myths and Myth Making in Tourism* (New York: John Wiley, 1996), 28.

44. See Koshar, *German Travel Cultures*, 11.

45. Suzanne K. Kaufman, "Selling Lourdes: Pilgrimage, Tourism, and the Mass-Marketing of the Sacred in Nineteenth-Century France," in *Being Elsewhere: Tourism, Consumer Culture, and Identity in Modern Europe and North America*, eds. Shelley Baranowski and Ellen Furlough (Ann Arbor: University of Michigan Press, 2001), 63–81, 64.

46. Kaufman, "Selling Lourdes," 70.

47. Justine Digance, "Pilgrimage at Contested Sites," 146.

48. Robert H. Stoddard, "Defining and Classifying Pilgrimages," in *Sacred Places, Sacred Spaces: The Geography of Pilgrimages*, eds. Robert H. Stoddard and Alan Morinis (Baton Rouge, La.: Louisiana State University, 1997), 41–60, 49.

49. Raymond Jonas, "Restoring a Sacred Center: Pilgrimage, Politics, and the Sacre Coeur," *Historical Reflections* 20, no. 1 (1994): 95–123, 101.

50. Eliza Fleischer, "The Tourist Behind the Pilgrim in the Holy Land," *International Journal of Hospitality Management* 19 (2000): 311–326, 311.

51. See Studstill, "Eliade, Phenomenology, and the Sacred."

52. BATr, Abt. 90, Nr. 132, 19 April 1937.

53. BATr, Abt. 90, Nr. 132, 21 April 1937.

54. BATr, Abt. 91, Nr. 223, 4.

55. BATr, Abt. 91, Nr. 223, 5.

56. BATr, Abt. 91, Nr. 225, 98.

57. BATr, Abt. 90, Nr. 101, 144.

58. BATr, Abt. 90, Nr. 102, 86, "Am 10. September beim Pfarrgottesdienste beobachtete ich jemanden, der das Bild der Hgl. Rockes voll Andacht in seinen Händen hielt. Er wischte sich wiederholt die Tränen aus der Augen."

59. BATr, Abt. 90, Nr. 106, 118, "Frl Zimmer wünscht mit Tränen in den Augen—den Hl. Rock des Erlösers berühren zu dürfen, ja bittet darum, wie ein tieffrommes Kind."

60. Cohen, "Who is a Tourist?," 542.

61. I explore this theme over two chapters in my book manuscript, *Moving Toward the German Sacred: Pilgrimage Space, 1832–1937*.

62. BATr, Abt. 91, Nr. 220, 40–49.

63. Daniel K. Connolly, "Imagined Pilgrimage in the Itinerary Maps of Matthew Paris," *The Art Bulletin* 81, no. 4 (1999): 598–622.

64. Connolly, "Imagined Pilgrimage," 598; Jean LeClercq, "Monachisme et pérégrination du IXe au XIIe siècle," *Studia Monastica* 3 (1961): 33–52.

65. Jean LeClercq, *The Love of Learning and the Desire for God: A Study of Monastic Culture*, trans. Catherine Misrahi (New York: Fordham University Press, 1982), 75.

66. LeClercq, *The Love of Learning*, 108.

67. Connolly, "Imagined Pilgrimage," 598.

68. Rappaport, *Ecology, Meaning and Religion*, 209.

69. BATr, Abt. 90 Nr. 173, 188–189, "Dem lb. Gott ist ja alles möglich, er kann mich auch aus der Ferne heilen, wie er den Knecht des Hauptmann Kornelius geheilt hat." This story appears in Matthew 8:5–13. Unfortunately, only Emma's request is in the BATr and not the Pilgrimage Committee's response. However, it is highly likely her ring was returned as the Pilgrimage Committee returned items sent with similar requests.

70. BATr, Abt. 91, Nr. 249a, 16.

71. BATr, Abt. 91, Nr. 249a, 15.

72. Robert Orsi, *History and Presence* (Cambridge, Mass.: Belknap Press of Harvard University Press, 2016), 9.

73. Hans Ulrich Gumbrecht, *The Production of Presence: What Meaning Cannot Convey* (Stanford: Stanford University Press, 2004).

Book Reviews

The Invention of Nature: Alexander von Humboldt's New World
BY ANDREA WULF
New York: Vintage Books, 2015

CAITLIN FINLAYSON

The extensively researched *The Invention of Nature* by Andrea Wulf chronicles the voyages of researcher Alexander von Humboldt and the impressive degree to which he inspired contemporary and later scientists, revolutionaries, and explorers. Wulf's book is largely a historical overview of Humboldt's life, beginning with his upbringing in Prussia and Berlin alongside his older brother, Wilhelm, and detailing his extensive travels across Europe, South America, and Russia. Wulf also explores the lives of scholars who were influenced by Humboldt's work even after his death, including conservationist George Perkins Marsh, biologist Ernst Haeckel, and naturalist John Muir. Humboldt's at times almost unbelievable travels and tribulations, including an investigation of electric eels in present-day Venezuela and an encounter with an anthrax outbreak along the Siberian Highway, transport the reader back to an age of exploration and discovery. Wulf's writing captures Humboldt's frenetic energy and excitement, and though the book is largely arranged chronologically, the structure of the chapters tends to meander, incorporating flashbacks and flash forwards, which likely mimics Humboldt's own musings. The illustrations and maps further serve to make the often forgotten Humboldt a tangible and accessible historical figure. In particular, the photograph of Humboldt's lecture notes, which is described as a "many-layered bricolage of thoughts, numbers, quotes and notes with no apparent order to anyone other than Humboldt" (230), presents him as a figure to whom many modern-day academics could relate.

In her book, Wulf sets out to "rediscover Humboldt, and to restore him to his rightful place in the pantheon of nature and science" (10) and the book largely succeeds in that endeavor. Wulf presents Humboldt as the singular inspiration behind a number of notable historical figures and thinkers, and the degree to which his truly extraordinary influence across science, politics, and the arts has largely been forgotten by the general public. In setting up a notion of Humboldt as a heroic visionary, however, Wulf's idealization of this undisputedly influential researcher overlooks some of the more problematic applications of Humboldt's works. If Humboldt was indeed "the reason why [Charles] Darwin was on the *Beagle*" (257), for example, and had "always loomed large in [Ernst] Haeckel's life" (353), then the influence that these men had on researchers like Friedrich Ratzel, whose conceptualization of the *Lebensraum* provided the scientific basis for German expansion in World War I, cannot be divorced from Humboldt's work. In *Cosmos*, Humboldt presents nature as "a 'living whole' where organisms were bound together in a 'net-like intricate fabric'" (290), which is not far removed from Ratzel's understanding of the organismic state. This is not to deny the impressive impact Humboldt's research had and continues to have on scholars worldwide, or to imply that Humboldt himself inspired German expansionism, but the presentation of Humboldt throughout Wulf's text glosses over the more controversial paradigms that followed his line of research.

At other times, Wulf overlooks the fact that while Humboldt's travels and explorations presented Europe with a wealth of new information, many of his "discoveries" were commonly known to indigenous groups. Humboldt is boldly described as a man who "gave us our concept of nature itself" (9), when some would argue that indigenous groups across the Americas and elsewhere had conceptualizations of the unified natural world and understood the importance of conservation long before Humboldt published his theories. Humboldt's legendary scaling of Chimborazo in the Andes, for example, is presented with exciting detail: "No one had ever come this high before, and no one had ever breathed such thin air" (2). While this might be true of Europeans, there is some evidence of indigenous groups scaling mountain peaks before the age of European exploration.

In addition, although the book's title might allude to the notion that Humboldt helped to create modern conceptualizations of "nature," nowhere does Wulf fully explore the "invention of nature" as an ontological endeavor, an ordering of the world into the categories of the "human" and "nature." This may be, perhaps, because Humboldt himself eschewed these kinds of distinctions, viewing humans as an interconnected part of the natural world. That said, the very notion of considering the impact of industrialization and agricultural development on the natural world, as the book explores, sets up a definition of "nature" that excludes these built environments and would have been an interesting philosophical angle for the reader to explore.

The Epilogue, in a way, is the most compelling section of Wulf's text particularly for modern researchers. Here, Wulf presents Humboldt's holistic approach to research as in direct contradiction to the highly specialized fields of modern scientists: "As scientists crawled into their narrow areas of expertise, dividing and further subdividing, they lost Humboldt's interdisciplinary methods and his concept of nature as a global force" (396). As an interdisciplinary journal, *Environment, Space, Place* is well-positioned to provide this multifaceted perspective that is often lacking in other research venues. Researchers who engage in mixed methods approaches or primarily qualitative methods within more scientific disciplines will similarly draw inspiration from Humboldt's work as it weaves narrative descriptions with experiments and observations. In the Epilogue, Wulf also connects Humboldt's legacy to the challenges of modern environmentalism, reiterating Humboldt's work as the revolutionary inspiration for numerous early naturalists and conservationists.

Overall, Wulf presents a comprehensive look into the life and travels of a man whose contributions have often been overlooked, but whose ideas about the relationship between people and nature has tremendous significance in modern times. Readers of *Environment, Space, Place* will appreciate Wulf's attention to historical detail, though they might also long for a more theoretical discussion of the implications of "inventing nature." Ultimately, Wulf manages to convey to readers the magnitude to which Humboldt's ideas have impacted our modern world and the sense of wonder with which Humboldt approached nature.

CAITLIN FINLAYSON is an assistant professor of geography at University of Mary Washington.

Connected: How Trains, Genes, Pineapples, Piano Keys, and a Few Disasters Transformed Americans at the Dawn of the Twentieth Century
BY STEVEN CASSEDY
Stanford: Stanford University Press, 2014

JOHN MARIANA

In 2010 the city of Colorado Springs was strapped for cash. Government officials announced that they would either have to raise revenue through increased taxation or cut public services—in some cases rather severely—including, perhaps, police and fire protection, and even more basic bits of municipal infrastructure. The city shut down one-third of residential streetlights and closed public restrooms. Citizens were outraged, but a majority of voters had recently defeated a proposed tax increase. It's tempting to suppose that the city was trying to teach its citizens a lesson: if you want public services, you have to be willing to pay for them. Colorado Springs is, and has been for some time now, a died-in-the-wool small-government, anti-tax-increase, fiscally conservative town. As Colorado Springs resident Bo Sharifi put it, "As soon as I hear government [say] 'Oh, we need more money' . . . I guess I kind of automatically assume there's probably some other things you could probably cut before firemen, policemen, city lights and that sort of thing."[1] On the surface, that seems reasonable. So . . . what comes to mind? How about food stamps? What about WIC? Of course these are *federal* services, not funded by Coloradans alone. There's government, and then there's government. Well, how about . . . well . . . what? Doesn't the government spend money on all sorts of things we could very easily do without? Perhaps. Isn't it part of *our* job to know or to decide which things these are?

If we don't trust government, even more obviously we don't trust it with our money, though we pretty clearly have no idea how public funds are actually allocated or spent. When asked whether he remembered the proposed tax increase that the city had voted against, Sharifi replied, "maybe." Bo and his wife were charged $125 to have their streetlight turned back on. Bo's wife Sara viewed this as extortion. "By shoveling out a hundred dollars to turn on a streetlight that we kind of felt was supposed to be on anyway, that it was giving them what they wanted," she said. *They who*? One resident wrote the city of Colorado Springs a check for $300 to turn the lights on for his entire neighborhood. City Councilwoman Jan Martin pointed out to him that the total cost to the individual Colorado Springs taxpayer to keep the streetlights on—*and* to fund the maintenance of public parks and medians, as well as community centers and pre-recession-level police and fire services—by approving the tax increase would have been: $200. He replied that he would never vote for a tax increase. In other words, as the reporter who covered the story (Robert Smith) observed, he would rather pay more to keep the streetlights on *in his own neighborhood* than to pay *for all city services combined*. Smith remarked that "Colorado Springs was stepping away from one of the things that we take for granted in most American cities: that we're all in it together—at least when it comes to basic services."[2]

As near as I can tell, this is the moral of Steven Cassedy's exceptionally timely *Connected*: that we're all in it together. For much of the book Cassedy merely traces the history of the emergence in the consciousness of ordinary Americans of the concept of the social network, but he is not so much talking about the notion of a network society as such, as I understand him. Or, at any rate, the network society as such is not really his main concern. He is talking about the idea of social, political, national, and ultimately global and universal human interconnectedness that was a distinct product of the complex networked structures (both concrete and abstract) that came to constitute modern American life in the twentieth century (and of course life pretty much everywhere), and about our understanding of ourselves as so networked.[3] On this level the book constitutes an extremely detailed, meticulous, and fascinating historical account of the construction (both intellectually and concretely) of a concept, or of a conception of ourselves, both as citizens and as human beings. But then this also serves as a basis for what I think is meant to be a reminder of the potential power and the hope implicit in this idea, as well as a reflection on its costs and on the potential benefits that could be thought to outweigh them.

If I seem hesitant to clearly and decisively assign a moral to Cassedy's work, this is only because he takes such a long time in arriving at it, and is so understated (if not downright evasive or vague) about drawing it himself, that I'm not confident he intended his book to be read this way. But it seems to me to be implicit in the work itself, and this strikes me as a message we sorely need right now. If Cassedy is right—that what emerged from the development of an awareness of a deeply and extensively networked self and society at the end of the nineteenth and the beginning of the twentieth centuries was a keen awareness of the dependence of the good of the individual on the good of society (or humanity) as a whole—then the question would seem to be: What happened to that idea? Where did it go? When, how, and why did we lose it?[4] It would take another history and perhaps another historian to tell that story (or maybe Cassedy himself will tell it in a follow-up book, with more overtly pointed and explicit social-critical aims and language). But I'm guessing that he wants us to feel the difference between the era which is the focus of his attention and our own era—to appreciate the loss or the severe attenuation of this idea.

It's perhaps tempting to think that Cassedy is simply wrong, and that there never really was any such idea to lose, but he makes an extremely compelling case for his historical and cultural and psychological claims. And in any event the questions of when, how, and why we lost this particular sort of understanding of ourselves as networked are questions that the book prompts, but not questions it intends to answer. And its call for us to remember the possibilities offered by such a self-understanding as beings deeply imbedded in networks (rather than shallowly imbedded as Twitter subscribers who are otherwise isolated consumers of social media promoting our own idealized self-conceptions as individuals) is compelling. As Cassedy himself puts it so beautifully on the final page of the book: "just as the distant stations and junctions on [a] rail network define any randomly chosen entryway into the network *as a kind of pure potentiality*—you can go there, it beckons you—so the myriad nodes on your several networks beckon you" (274; italics mine). In reminding us of the history of the development of our understanding of ourselves as deeply networked, Cassedy seems to be hoping to rekindle some of the spirit of the times in which this understanding took shape.

He divides his discussion into three sections, which represent ever-widening circles (or expanding webs) of social interconnectedness, beginning with what he calls (in the second chapter) "the biological self." Cassedy tells us that Americans first came to understand themselves as networked internally—as biological networks consisting of a variety of reciprocally interacting systems of sub-networks—and thus as networked externally to other human beings as a consequence of the realization of the reciprocal interdependence of the health of the individual and the health of the community at large. In other words, society itself could be conceived as a sort of organism in macrocosm. (Cassedy's point here is an historical one, but in the context of the larger project of the book he seems to be taking aim directly at anti-vaxxers and other advocates of opt-out politics.) Of course, analogies between individuals as organic systems and cities, states, and countries (and buildings, and ships) as networks were hardly new. Such analogies have been around for centuries, if not millennia. What was new was not merely the modern form of the social network that is characteristic of mass society, but the understanding of this reciprocal relationship of networked interdependence as part of a *scientific* conception of humankind, as scientifically implying the unity (and thus the unification) of all humanity.

Of course all of this took place against the backdrop of the growing acceptance of Darwinian evolutionary theory, and though Cassedy discusses the religious basis for the rejection of Darwinism that grew up in the latter half of the nineteenth century, he convincingly argues that the die had already been cast. The impact of Darwinism across the sciences could not help but transform our understanding of ourselves as living creatures, and as human beings. Heredity bound us each to each, across all humanity, back through all past generations and forward through all the generations yet to come. According to Cassedy, what emerged in this context from the formulation of a mature cellular theory and the discovery of germs was not only a richer understanding of the causes and courses of communicable illness but a new form of awareness of ourselves as simultaneously *the occupants, architects, and products of networks.* This awareness insinuated itself into the minds of ordinary Americans through public health campaigns that drew their organizing principles directly from the sciences. Here we have the earliest signs of the emergence of a truly new form of technocratic social management, driven by science and fundamentally secular and pragmatic in spirit.

Interestingly, Cassedy develops this story within the context of a discussion of some rather ambitious nineteenth century speculations on the possibility of the indefinite prolongation of the individual human life span. Scientists, and before very long even lay-people, could already see that advancements in our understanding of health and disease were beginning to defy the actuaries, and that not only could average Americans reasonably expect to live longer than their grandparents, one could also reasonably expect simply to survive into adulthood in the first place. But in the public's mind, the science could be read as implying the possibility of indefinite survival, barring misadventure. This optimism, which persisted and even gained momentum through the first decades of the twentieth century, would seem puzzling given that tuberculosis, and later influenza and war, continued to claim millions of American lives. But Cassedy locates the source of such American optimism squarely in the concept of the network, which would explain its persistence in the face of what would otherwise seem to be some pretty discouraging realities. Then as now, Americans base their faith in progress on the indomitable power of the network to solve social problems and cure social diseases. Hence our unshakable optimism: there will always be problems; but we believe that for any social problem—no matter how large and seemingly intractable—there is a collectivist solution. Here, and in a number of other places in the book, Cassedy's work rises to the level of some of the very best American historical and historiographical scholarship, offering us both a window on and a critique of part of our conception of ourselves as it was taking shape.

Cassedy concludes his discussion of the biological self with a rather detailed examination of nineteenth century neurophysiological theories of mind and the challenges they faced at the time, both technical and philosophical. In particular, Cassedy focuses on the criticisms of reductive neurophysiology then being advanced by Henri Bergson. Bergson might seem an odd choice of subject, but strange as it may seem, Cassedy reveals that Bergson had a following even in America (or at least among New Yorkers, at any rate) that would nearly rival Lisztomania in its frenziedness. But the real headline here has to do with the relation between rival theories of mind and the development of a universal system of standardized time, and Bergson's philosophy was positioned right at the very point of their intersection. Here's where the book, and its larger argument, really gets started, and for my money the middle section is far and away the most fascinating part of the entire text—though it's a bit heavy-going.

It seemed to many scientists and philosophers at the time (as it also later seemed to the Positivists of the Vienna Circle, and to Bertrand Russell for a time) that if we take a reductive approach to mental phenomena, viewing them as nothing more than neurophysiological events in the brain, this meant that we could not say definitively whether space and time are mind-independently real. This is because the unit of study is the neuron, not the world outside the mind, and nerve endings simply register stimulations; so, we have no way of knowing whether the sources of stimuli are in fact represented to us in our minds as they actually are in themselves. Bergson rejected all this, and concluded that though space is mind-independent, time is not. This is because *actions* take place in time, and constitute syncretic wholes that cannot be meaningfully subdivided, as space can be subdivided. But not only had the assumption of the divisibility of time taken firm hold on human thought by the nineteenth century, specific divisions and subdivisions came to organize human life and human activity across the globe, mostly as a result of the need to coordinate railway timetables. And so spatialized time and temporalized space become the philosophically contested territories that dominate much of our thinking about the relation between mind and world, self and environment, throughout the twentieth century, and emerge at the dawn of the century as two additional, larger-scale networks within which we locate ourselves as socially coordinated beings—as, again, both products and architects. Cassedy unfolds the conceptual connections between time, space, self, our internal mental and biological networks, and the external networks of railroads and wristwatches in a way that is almost as much poetry as it is good scholarship.

From there Cassedy proceeds through a discussion of the subsequent development of the modern form of internationalized commerce, including universal standardized timekeeping, that would revolutionize both the global economy and the material prospects of ordinary Americans, who could then enjoy such exotic delicacies as canned Hawaiian pineapples and Congolese ivory. The picture that Cassedy paints is both familiar and depressing, presaging the end of the era of colonialism and the rise of new forms of global economic exploitation. And so we are set to witness all of the resulting conflicts of the twentieth century. But Cassedy's claim is that the American awareness and understanding of the emerging global economy as a system of reciprocally interdependent networks gave rise to a keen awareness of social injustice in all its forms, which later came to characterize the major social movements of the early-to-mid twentieth century. He concludes with a discussion of how even American religious institutions were swept up in these movements and came to see their missions as being as much about the here-and-now of politics aimed at alleviating material suffering as about ultimate spiritual salvation.

I should say, however, that Cassidy never really makes plain just what exactly he means by a network; and he never explicitly defines the network concept anywhere in the book. Throughout most of the text I could only conclude that what he meant by a network is a *complex adaptive system* (or worse, merely a cluster or web or framework of associations), in which case his conclusions would hardly be either surprising or deeply revealing—except to the extent that he would have established a plausible account (from scientific discovery to media dissemination to social efforts at confronting the unwanted, unintended effects of complex adaptive systems and managing them) of the context and conditions of the emergence of the modern concept of the social network. But Cassedy clearly means something else by a network, or rather by the idea of understanding oneself as occupying a network or being self-consciously a member of a network, or of *being networked*, and the nearest I can come to expressing this idea without giving it any specific political inflection (as Cassedy himself declines to do) would be to describe it as: *a sense of solidarity*.[5]

The notion of solidarity would seem to belong to socialist politics, but the basic idea is essentially humanistic. As Noam Chomsky points out, solidarity at bottom simply consists of, or emerges from, recognizing oneself as being united in common cause with (and so networked to) others. And when those others are *any* others, solidarity encompasses all humanity. It might seem surprising (or mistaken) to think that such a feeling of solidarity emerged during, and characterized, the period of American history just prior to and continuing through and after the First World War, given what happened at mid-century. But this is just one of the surprising insights of Cassedy's study. The notions of solidarity and of social (even universal) justice that Cassedy employs are often thought by those on both sides of our political spectrum to be the enemies of wealth and power, and so they are in some versions. But Cassedy shows us—or reminds us—that this is neither necessary nor inevitable. This is another of his insights, and this sort of reminder could perhaps help us to think our way out of our present socialist-fascist impasse.

Cassedy notes in more than one place in the book that the cost of being networked is a loss of, or a relatively significant curtailment or contraction of, the sphere of individual autonomy. We all know this quite well already, but Cassedy isn't really talking about the sort of loss of autonomy that is simply a feature of any complex, bureaucratically managed and organized mass society. His point is not Kafkian; in fact, if anything it's precisely the reverse. His point is that we suffer a loss of autonomy in the sense that we must in some measure (if not in large measure) sacrifice ourselves to the collective. Structurally speaking, we have no other choice. Cassedy says repeatedly throughout the book that once you're in the network, you're in, whether you like it or not, and that there's no getting out. Here is the one place in the book where Cassedy seems almost downright polemical, clearly favoring a network of individuals in solidarity (or, as he puts it, "a network of mutual aid and cooperation") to an atomized society of isolated individuals united only in their commitment to consumption, or a tribal society of warring factions. "If the networked human being has sacrificed some measure of autonomy in return for a host of networks," he says, "maybe the networks bring material and social benefits that outweigh the loss of autonomy" (273).

The history of modernity seems to be one long story of occasional bursts of progress in the direction of something like a universal concept of justice, separated by painful, extended, often disastrous and hideous, periods of regression into old forms of tribalism. And there are times where Cassedy could perhaps be accused of adhering to some sort of naïve modernization theory or theory of historical necessity, or that he is carried away by his own optimism about the ability of networks to save us from ourselves. He often presents the developments he traces as though they were inevitable and neglects to explain the failure of competing forms of social self-awareness to carry the day, or to discuss or explore the reasons for, and the extent to which, we've lost the sense of solidarity that he seems to endorse. But Cassedy can,

I think, be excused for these oversights, given the oceans of ink that have been spilt on such subjects by other historians, philosophers, and critical theorists. And in any event, I think that his aim is in part precisely to suggest that a spirit of networked solidarity can exist alongside wealth and power and without revolution, but with "the kind of pure potentiality" that "beckons" us to imagine a brighter future for us all.

JOHN MARIANA is a professor of philosophy at the College of the Canyons.

NOTES

1. *This American Life.* "What Kind of Country?—Act Three: Do You Want a Wake-Up Call?" Episode 459. Hosted by Ira Glass. Report by Robert Smith. Chicago Public Media, March 2, 2012. Transcript: https://www.thisamericanlife.org/radio-archives/episode/459/transcript.
2. Ibid.
3. This is what makes his title so appropriate. The keyword here is *connected*, though he relies heavily and extensively on the network concept throughout his discussion.
4. I can't argue for this here, but it seems to me to be beyond question that we have indeed lost the idea of ourselves as networked in the sense that Cassedy has in mind—or at any rate that such an understanding of ourselves in relation to society is generally regarded as outdated or naïve, or both, and impossible under our current circumstances. The case of the Colorado Springs budget crisis is just one example. One contributing cause of our loss of the idea of universal solidarity as an ideal was, however, oddly enough, the rise of identity politics, which emerged in the early part of the twentieth century and gradually took its contemporary shape during the decades following World War II. The critical philosophical project of the theorization of identity politics has given rise to a powerful challenge to a univocal concept of global justice, in favor of a variety of pluralist forms. Whether or not this is (or ultimately can be) part of a unifying system of juridical arbitration of disputes between identity groups is itself an issue that is hotly contested. In one sense it might seem (at least superficially) that identity politics could thus imply or even require a retreat into certain forms of tribalism, but I'm not really in a position here to take a stand on the issue one way or the other. Suffice it to say that it's a bit of a shame that Cassedy's discussion, as a historical study, doesn't really leave room for a treatment of these matters. But such a treatment would probably require a whole other book.
5. In the words of Felix Adler, quoted by Cassedy: "I, as an individual, am also inextricably linked up backward and forward with those who come before and those who are to come after. I cannot take myself out of this web. The task laid upon human society as a whole is also laid upon me. I am a conscious thread in the fabric that is weaving, conscious in a general way of the pattern to be woven" (239).

Gendered Geographies in Puerto Rican Culture:
Spaces, Sexualities, Solidarities
BY RADOST RANGELOVA
North Carolina Studies in the Romance Languages and Literatures
Chapel Hill: University of North Carolina Press, 2016

RAE ROSENBERG

As Rangelova's title implies, her book *Gendered Geographies in Puerto Rican Culture* provides a unique and significant intervention in geography by using gender and sexuality as the linchpins of an analysis of labor, citizenship, and nation in Puerto Rico. It is encouraging to read a feminist geographical text that so strongly commits to weaving together ideas of gender and sexuality with race, labor, and the effects of colonialism and imperialism. In particular, Rangelova provides readers an effective and intriguing analysis of how various Puerto Rican spaces are shaped and informed by women and the complex networks of gendered and sexual power that they negotiate.

Readers are brought through an effectively-crafted argument about how everyday spaces uncover forms of labor, violence, and resistance that are typically ignored in geography. As Rangelova explains, the book aims to analyze "gendered geographies and forms of emotional labor, and the spaces of possibility that they generate within the material and the symbolic spaces of the factory, the family house, the beauty salon and the brothel" (11) in Puerto Rico. She does so by examining the different forms and sites of women's physical, domestic, and emotional labor in these spaces as they have manifested in Puerto Rican literature and film. While not a trained geographer, Rangelova utilizes space effectively to examine how Puerto Rican women's bodies, experiences, subjectivities, actions, and social positions have (re)constructed the links between nation, gender, race, and sexuality. For Rangelova, exploring these spaces illustrates how Puerto Rican women "use space, and the queering of space, as a strategy to resist marginalization and oppression imposed by limited definitions of the nation in their specific contexts" (33).

Rangelova centralizes power in her analysis, attempting to "uncover the ways in which women use certain spaces to turn patriarchy upon itself, and to exercise agency in the creation of different relations of power in spaces that they make inaccessible to patriarchal order" (22). Rangelova draws upon materialist feminism and the work of Massey, Duncan, McKittrick, and Wright to prioritize the intersections of gender with race, class, and sexuality, in order to interrogate how space and nation are cultivated through these axes of power and identity. Following feminist geographical arguments, Rangelova understands space to be transformable, unfixed, and contested, and in doing so disrupts the ways in which labor is often considered and theorized spatially—notably void of women and feminized forms of labor (23–24).

A large portion of Rangelova's insistence upon analyzing power rests on race, and writing race and racism into spatial analyses of women's lives. For Rangelova, race is fundamental for feminist geographical analysis, and "its significance calls for a need to expand the theoretical conception of materialist feminism to include a broader understanding of the significance of race in women's material conditions and political agency" (27). In the Puerto Rican context, Rangelova reads the traces of anti-Black racism through the literary and cinematic texts that comprise of her analysis. For example, Rangelova explores how race informs how women are often mapped onto the urban landscape in ways that "clearly define female (often black) sexuality as undesirable and only allowed in spaces regulated by law" (160). Colonial policies that regulated brothels to particular locations in urban space were, as she argues, racialized processes. The legacy of slavery in Puerto Rico left many Black and Afro-Puerto Rican women living in poverty and excluded from access to work, leading many to engage in sex work (158). As "the desire to construct a white, patriarchal Puerto Rican nation" (156–57) became more strongly enforced by Spanish colonialists, these spaces of women of color's labor were spatially isolated in the Puerto Rican urban fabric, and shamed in Puerto Rican institutional and nation-building discourses. As Rangelova explains, "The control of urban space and of the spaces of prostitution was conditioned by a set of prejudices that informed the effort to categorize racial, class and sexual traits as undesirable in the Puerto Rican national discourse" (157).

Rangelova incorporates queerness into her writing by understanding it as an act of disruption in response to various forms of power, as well as same-gender desire between women in Puerto Rican literature and cinematic discourses. Apart from the stories of same-gender desire and teasing apart the texts to reveal homoerotic interactions between Puerto Rican women, Rangelova's use of queer remains largely abstract throughout the book. It would have proven an interesting and dynamic use of queerness to see Rangelova explore it as more than a sexual political position, but also as a gendered political position grounded in the survival of queer Puerto Ricans. Throughout the book, I wondered how a discussion of Puerto Rican transgender women's spaces may or may not emerge in Puerto Rican film and literature, and how this could contribute a more nuanced understanding of Puerto Rican women's gendered geographies. Rangelova also utilizes sexuality to bridge conversations of sexual citizenship with the Puerto Rican city, and Puerto Rican nationalism more broadly. In the literary and cinematic discourses analyzed by Rangelova, the national imaginary emerges as a sexualized and gendered discourse that denies sexual others, such as sex workers, full citizenship (159). While this discussion is particularly important when analyzing the effects of power and oppression, readers of *Environment, Space, Place* may find themselves wanting to see these ideas elaborated upon throughout the book.

Yet part of what makes Rangelova's book such a significant addition to geography is her use of spatial analysis, and in particular how she incorporates discussions about how women's labor and acts of everydayness inform the Puerto Rican city. In considering domestic spaces as necessarily central to the makeup of urban space, Rangelova relates Puerto Rican urbanity with women's sexuality and forms of power such as racism, colonialism, and patriarchy. Invoking the writing of Lefebvre, Rangelova explores and emphasizes the power of everydayness in Puerto Rican urbanity. In her analysis of the short story "Pilar, tus rizos," Rangelova argues that the beauty salon simultaneously reaffirms and also fosters resistance to patriarchy, and in the story comes to represent the city as "a dynamic and negotiated construction of multiple axes of power" (143). In the last scene where Pilar, the main character, takes a phone call from her husband, the space of the beauty salon and the identities within it are transformed through a connection to Pilar's home and husband, ultimately "expos[ing] and critiqu[ing] patriarchal models of gender and sexuality" (143). Rangelova applies the notion of everydayness as transformative and subversive to the conditions of Puerto Rican women as they are represented in literary and cinematic texts, illustrating how domestic spheres "become examples of the malleability of urban space, of its constructed nature and the need to think of it as a site of struggle, contradiction, and constant negotiation" (143). In providing this exploration of the power of mundane acts of living in urban spaces, Rangelova challenges the ways in which urban theory has erased places largely occupied by women, and the experiences of women, by illustrating their relevance to understandings of cities and how they inform the construction of urban space.

The powerful contributions of this book ultimately rest in its clear and effective use of feminist geographical scholarship to dismantle the dichotomies of public and private, domestic and public, in order to continue uncovering the many ways in which women's experiences, subjectivities, and resistances impact geography. Rangelova's book not only offers critical insight into realms where women's labor has been invisibilized and relegated as forgettable, but also serves as a powerful gesture to remind readers that domestic spaces are also working spaces, and that sex, family, and emotional labor is also work. *Gendered Geographies in Puerto Rican Culture* challenges the forms of masculinized rationality and masculine gaze that have been built into geographic scholarship, and Rangelova provides readers with critical, interesting, and unique writing that represents a hopeful direction of feminist geographical work.

RAE ROSENBERG is a PhD student in geography at York University (Toronto).